Read All About It

Book 2

Lori Howard

OXFORD
UNIVERSITY PRESS

Oxford University Press
198 Madison Avenue, New York, NY 10016 USA
Great Clarendon Street, Oxford OX2 6DP England

Oxford New York
Auckland Bangkok Buenos Aires Cape Town Chennai
Dar es Salaam Delhi Hong Kong Istanbul Karachi Kolkata
Kuala Lumpur Madrid Melbourne Mexico City Mumbai Nairobi
São Paulo Shanghai Singapore Taipei Tokyo Toronto

with an associated company in *Berlin*

OXFORD is a trademark of Oxford University Press.

Library of Congress Cataloging-in-Publication Data

Howard Lori (Lori B.)
 Read all about it, Book 2 /Lori Howard.
 p. cm – (Oxford picture dictionary series)
 includes index.
 Summary: Presents short readings with questions for thought and
 discussion
 ISBN 0-19-435224-2 (pbk.: alk.paper)
 1. English language–Textbooks for foreign speakers. 2. Readers.
 [1. English language–Textbooks for foreign speakers. 2. Readers.]
 I. Title. II. Series.

 PE1128.H627 2000
 428.2′4–dc21   99-052335

Editorial Manager: Susan Lanzano
Senior Editor: Amy Cooper
Content Editors: Nan Clarke/Debbie Sistino
Senior Production Editor: Robyn F. Clemente
Production Editor: Janice Baillie
Art Director: Lynn Luchetti
Designer: Nona Renter
Production Layout: Maj-Britt Ilagsted
Art Buyer/Picture Researcher: Stacy Godlesky
Production Manager: Abram Hall
Production Coordinator: Shanta Persaud

Cover design by Mark C.Kellogg and Shelley Hinumelstein

Printing (last digit): 10 9 8 7 6 5 4 3

Printed in Hong Kong

Illustrations and realia by: Eliot Bergman, Annie Bissett, Chuck
Boie/Art Factory, Uldis Klavins, Joe LeMonnier, Zina Saunders,
Stacey Schuett, Carol Strebel, Anna Veltfort

*The publishers would like to thank the following for their
permission to reproduce photographs:* Jack Anthony;
David Lissy, Bob Martin/Allsport; Paul Chiasson, Stringer,
Les Walker/AP/Wide World Photos; Jorg Brockman;
Michael S. Yamashita/Corbis; Greg Gibson/Corbis/Bettman;
Green Glass USA; Robert Baker/HFHI; NASA; Mike Chew,
Michael H. Dunn, Mark A. Johnson, Rob Lewine, Chris and
Donna McLaughlin, Mug Shots, Alon Reininger/Contact Press;
David Stoecklein/The Stock Market

The publishers would also like to thank the following for their help:
"Knoxville, Tennessee" from *Black Feeling, Black Talk,
    Black Judgment*, by Nikki Giovanni. Copyright © 1968,
    1970 by Nikki Giovanni. By Permission of William Morrow
    Company, Inc.
Blondie, by Dean Young & Stan Drake
    Copyright © 1995, King Features Syndicate, Inc.
    Reprinted with special permission of North America
    Syndicate.
"Casual Friday" Cartoon
    From the *Wall Street Journal*. By permission of Cartoon
    Feature Syndicate.
"Casual Friday" graph based on information from Society for
    Human Resource Management and Levi Strauss & Co.
    Used with permission.
"Coolhunters" © Copyright NPR® 1997 The news report by
    NPR's Deborah Amos was originally broadcast on
    National Public Radio's "All Things Considered®" on
    March 20, 1997 and is used with the permission of
    National Public Radio, Inc. Any unauthorized duplication
    is strictly prohibited.

References
Brill, Marlene Targ, *Let Women Vote!*, Brookfield, Connecticut,
    The Millbrook Press, Inc., 1996.
Daily News Record
Keenan, Sheila, *Scholastic Encyclopedia of Women in the
    United States*. Copyright © 1996 by Scholastic Inc.
    All rights reserved.Published by Scholastic Inc.
McMullin, Mary (Series Editor), *Teacher Training Through
    Video: Cooperative Learning*. White Plains, NY: Longman
    Publishing Group, 1993.
Stille, Darlene R., *Extraordinary Women Scientists*.
    Copyright © 1995 by Children's Press, Inc.
    All rights reserved.
U.S. Department of Labor, *Occupational Outlook Handbook*,
    1998-99 Edition.

TO THE TEACHER

Welcome to Oxford's *Read All About It* series.

Read All About It 2 is a collection of engaging articles, stories, and poems for adult and young adult students of English as a Second or Foreign Language at a high-beginning level to low-intermediate level.

Each of the twelve thematic units in this book contains two high-interest readings based on authentic materials, including news stories, magazine articles, biographies, folktales, and poetry. The readings and activities in each unit focus on one topic such as housing, food, or clothing. This gives students the opportunity to read, listen, speak, and write about one topic in depth and to reinforce and expand their knowledge of related vocabulary. A wide variety of pre-reading, reading, and post-reading activities gives students numerous opportunities to develop cultural awareness as well as problem solving and critical thinking skills. Students will also build reading fluency through the practice of skills such as predicting, skimming, scanning, guessing meaning from context, inferring, and comprehension.

Read All About It 2 is interactive. Students are encouraged to interact with the text by using their knowledge and experience to help them understand the readings. Students can also interact with each other as they complete the many thought-provoking pair and group activities that accompany the readings.

Read All About It 2 is designed to be flexible and adaptable to the needs of classes and individual students. It can be used as a core reader, as a reading supplement, or for independent study. An accompanying audio tape includes recordings of the readings.

Students who are also using *The Oxford Picture Dictionary* will find that *Read All About It 2* helps bring the *Dictionary* vocabulary to life. Each unit in *Read All About It 2* focuses on the same topic and vocabulary as the corresponding unit in *The Oxford Picture Dictionary* and incorporates vocabulary from other units as well. Students who use *Read All About It 2* will gain confidence in their reading ability and learn that they can understand what they read without knowing every word. The strategies they learn will help them enjoy reading and encourage them to read more.

Tour of a Unit

TALK ABOUT IT, usually led by the teacher, is aimed at introducing the topic, motivating the students, and encouraging them to share their prior knowledge about it. The open-ended activities presented in this section allow students of varying abilities to participate and benefit. They can share their personal experiences through guided discussions with classmates.

READ ABOUT IT includes pre-reading, reading, and post-reading activities. Although many activities direct students to work in pairs or small groups, almost all of the activities can be done individually.

Before You Read asks students to gather more specific information about the upcoming passage just as competent readers do. Students look at illustrations or photos that accompany the reading, as well as the title and headings, and make predictions about the reading. New vocabulary is introduced in context and, in many cases, is evident in the captions of the pictures. *Before You Read* can be teacher-led or done individually and then discussed with the whole group.

While You Read focuses students on the reading and asks them to reflect on their pre-reading predictions as they read silently. Students are not expected to understand every word; they should be encouraged to read for the general meaning and to use context clues and their background knowledge to aid comprehension. Readings increase slightly in length and complexity as students progress. Activities include:

▶ *What did you read?* Students are asked to identify the main idea of the reading.

▶ *Read again* provides students with a second opportunity to read the whole passage or parts of the passage silently, focusing on a set of comprehension questions.

▶ *Show you understand* asks students to demonstrate their comprehension of the passage in a variety of ways such as using vocabulary in context, categorizing, sequencing ideas, and making inferences.

▶ *Talk more about it* invites students to relate the material they have read to their own experience and knowledge and use it to discuss ideas, history, and/or culture. Depending on their level of fluency, they may offer short answers or delve more deeply into the questions with longer discussions.

After You Read helps students to further develop their reading skills and vocabulary. Students practice writing, which supports and reinforces the reading. Depending on the time available, these activities can be either done in class or assigned for homework.

READ MORE ABOUT IT offers an opportunity for students to read further about the same topic. Shorter than READ ABOUT IT, it is similar in format and includes many of the same kinds of activities.

Special Features

Teacher's Notes
Teacher's Notes include general information about using this book, specific information about each unit, and suggested extension activities.

Answer Key
A removable Answer Key is available for individuals to check their work. However, when students are working in pairs or small groups, they should be encouraged to check their answers with each other to maximize peer interaction. This flexibility makes *Read All About It 2* useful in classroom, laboratory, and home settings alike.

Word List
A unit-by-unit word list provides *The Oxford Picture Dictionary* page references for vocabulary used in this book, so that students who have the *Dictionary* can use it for support. Teachers can also use the list to determine which words in the readings appear in the *Dictionary*.

Remember the Words
A personal vocabulary diary helps students learn new words of their choice.

I hope you and your students enjoy *Read All about It 2*, and I welcome your comments and ideas.

Write to me at:

> Oxford University Press, ESL Department
> 198 Madison Avenue
> New York, New York 10016

Lori Howard

Author's Acknowledgments

The author would like to thank the following people for their very helpful reviews of the manuscript: Jose Olavo de Amorim, Steven Blakesly, Stephen Sloan, Connie Tucker, Zirka Voronka, Laura Webber

The contributions of the following people are deeply appreciated:
Nan Clarke, Editor, who put heart and soul into this book.
Debbie Sistino, Editor, whose attitude and suggestions were always just right.
Amy Cooper, Senior Editor, who was always there to help and whose wonderful work on Book 1 set the stage for Book 2.
Justin Hartung for his kindness and his tireless work on the many details of this project.
Susan Lanzano, Editorial Manager, who had confidence in me from the outset of this project.

Special thanks to my husband, Greg Wolff, whose help and encouragement made this book possible, and to our children, Eric and Lindsay, for their patience and support. Much gratitude goes to Jayme Adelson-Goldstein and Norma Shapiro for their invaluable suggestions throughout the development of the manuscript and their unwavering support.

Many thanks to Julie Bernard for being there for me in so many ways.

Sincere thanks to my students, colleagues, friends, and family members, especially David Thorman, Elsie Lee, Bill Small, Joanne Low, and the students at the Chinatown/North Beach Campus of City College of San Francisco; Inez Cohen; Jan Schrumpf; Craig Chambers; Kris Beale; Sue Warhaftig.

Thanks also go to the following individuals and organizations who provided their expertise: The reference librarians of the San Francisco and Mill Valley Public Libraries and the Marin County Free Libraries; Randall W. Scott, Librarian, Comic Art Collection, Michigan State University Libraries; The Fashion Institute of Design & Merchandising Library, San Francisco Campus; Diane Monteil, LAc; Ellen Mettler, LAc; Stuart Kutchins, OMD, LAc; Jean-Maurice Filion, Director of Linguistic Services, Canada Post; Arthur R. Jackson, Green Glass USA; Nancy Soreide, National Weather Service; Matt Sittel, Research Assistant, Center for Ocean-Atmospheric Prediction Studies; National Oceanic and Atmospheric Administration; Lisa Kim, Traffic Manager, KGO Radio, San Francisco.

This book is dedicated to my mom and dad, Esse and Len Wolff, two loving and courageous people, and to my father, William Lesly Howard, an inventor, a poet, a dreamer, and a great storyteller.

CONTENTS

TALK ABOUT IT

A. Work with a partner. Look at the pictures. Circle the answers.

"If at first you don't succeed, try, try again."

1. What is the woman doing?	**a.** She's building a house.	**b.** She's putting up a tent.
2. How many times does she try?	**a.** She tries once.	**b.** She tries more than once.
3. Why is she successful?	**a.** She does it alone.	**b.** She gets help.

B. Think about these questions. Then ask and answer the questions with your partner.

1. What does the caption under the cartoon mean?

2. The woman needed help from her friends to succeed. What else do people need to succeed? Name three things.

3. What was your last success? What helped you succeed?

4. Who is the most successful person you know? What helped him or her succeed? What can you learn from him or her?

Before You Read

Look at the pictures. Look at the title of the reading. Guess the answers to the questions.

1. What kind of class does the man teach?

   a. cooking   **b.** math   **c.** Spanish

2. The banner on the wall says, "Ganas...that's all you need." What does the Spanish word *ganas* mean?

   a. money   **b.** friends   **c.** desire

3. What does this teacher think the students need to succeed?

   _____

Read this biography. Think about your guesses while you read.

A Special Teacher

Jaime Escalante stood in front of his class. He was wearing an apron and a chef's hat. There were three apples on his desk, and he was cutting them into pieces with a sharp knife. But he wasn't teaching cooking. He was teaching math. Mr. Escalante wanted his students to learn fractions, so he was cutting the apples into thirds, fourths, and eighths.

From 1974 to 1991 Mr. Escalante was a teacher at Garfield High School in East Los Angeles. Most of his students came from low-income Latino families. They didn't have much money, and they spoke Spanish at home. Some people didn't think these students could learn much. But Mr. Escalante knew they could learn. He tried to make learning fun. He gave them math problems about sports, dating, shopping, and other things the teenagers liked. This helped the students be successful. They quickly learned math!

Mr. Escalante wanted his students to love learning. He wanted them to have a strong desire or wish to learn. The Spanish word for a strong desire is *ganas*. Mr. Escalante told his students that, with *ganas*, they could do anything. But telling them wasn't enough. He had to show them.

He began to teach them calculus, an advanced type of math. He wanted them to take a calculus test that only the top 3% of students in the United States take. The test is difficult, so Mr. Escalante helped his students study every day for a whole year. Before school, during school, after school, and even on Saturday mornings, they studied calculus together.

In the spring of 1982 Mr. Escalante's students took the test. They all did well and passed! What a success! But some people thought they cheated. They thought the students copied the correct answers from other students' papers. So the students took the test again. And they passed again! The students proved to themselves and their community that, with *ganas*, they could do anything. With desire, hard work, and the help of their great teacher, they succeeded.

▶ *What did you read?*

Circle the main idea.

a. Jaime Escalante teaches math.

b. With hard work anyone can learn.

c. Calculus is difficult to learn.

▶ *Read again*

**Are these sentences true? Find the answers in the reading. Circle *yes* or *no*.
Check your answers with a partner.**

1. Mr. Escalante taught cooking.	yes	(no)
2. Some people thought the students couldn't learn.	yes	no
3. Mr. Escalante made learning fun.	yes	no
4. He used sports to teach math.	yes	no
5. The students studied calculus for two years.	yes	no
6. The students cheated on the test.	yes	no
7. The students passed the test twice.	yes	no

▶ *Show you understand*

**Put these sentences in order. Number them from 1–5. Then retell the story
to your partner. Add other details you remember.**

_____ **a.** They took the test again and passed again.

__1__ **b.** Mr. Escalante was a math teacher at Garfield High School.

_____ **c.** So he began to teach them calculus.

_____ **d.** The students took a calculus test and passed.

_____ **e.** He wanted his students to have a strong desire to learn.

▶ *Talk more about it*

Think about these questions. Then discuss your ideas.

> **1.** How did Jaime Escalante make learning fun? Why did he do that?
>
> **2.** What helped the students succeed?
>
> **3.** What do you want to be successful at? What can you do to make
> it happen? Whose help do you need?

After You Read

▶ *Words, words, words*

A. Read the sentences. What do the <u>underlined</u> words mean? Write the letters of the correct meanings in the blanks. Use clues in the reading to help you, and write the clues you find.

    a. Latin American   **c.** wish   **e.** succeeded

    b. were not honest   ~~**d.**~~ poor

                                                 Clues

  _d_ **1.** Most of the students came from
          <u>low-income</u> Latino families.   They didn't have much money.

      2. Most of the students came from
          low-income <u>Latino</u> families.

      3. He wanted them to have a strong <u>desire</u>
          to learn.

      4. They all did well and <u>passed</u>!

      5. But some people thought they <u>cheated</u>.

B. Study the word family. Look at the examples. Then fill in the blanks with the correct words.

Word Family	Examples
succeed *verb*	With desire, hard work, and the help of their great teacher, they *succeeded*.
success *noun*	What a *success*!
successful *adjective*	This helped the students be *successful*.

Arturo Soriano wants to be a _____ artist. He will _____

because he is studying hard. His _____ will make his family proud.

▶ *Write*

Write a paragraph about your best teacher on your own paper. Use these questions and the example to help you. Who was your best teacher? What did he or she teach? Why was he or she a good teacher?

    Mrs. Iwataki was my best teacher. She taught English as a Second Language at the adult school. Her class was fun, and we learned a lot. She made us feel successful.

Before You Read

Look at the picture. Look at the title of the reading. Guess the answers to the questions. Circle them.

1. Does this reading take place now?   yes   no
2. Does this boy like school?   yes   no
3. Is he a good student?   yes   no

While You Read

Read this page from an imaginary diary. Think about your guesses while you read.

A Difficult Beginning

 October 20, 1889

Miss Koch came into the classroom at exactly 8:30 this morning. We all stood up and were quiet. She greeted us and wrote, "page number 101" on the chalkboard. We sat down on our hard, uncomfortable chairs. Then we opened our thick books and began to study.

A few minutes later I had a question, so I raised my hand. As usual Miss Koch said, "Not now." I was very frustrated because she never answers my questions. So I asked John. Miss Koch heard me talking. She told me to write "I will not talk in class" on the chalkboard 50 times. I was angry, but I apologized to her. Then I wrote the words on the board. But I wasn't thinking about talking in class. I was thinking about how much I hate school.

I walked home alone. It was cloudy and gray. It looked like it might rain, but I didn't care. It was Friday and I couldn't wait for the party to begin. On Fridays our friends always come to our house. They play music and read poetry. Father reads aloud from my favorite books. They all discuss the news. I love to listen to them talk about new inventions like the telephone and the electric light. And best of all, my parents and their friends answer all my questions.

I know I don't learn much from school, but I learn a lot from these evenings at home. My teacher thinks I will never be successful, but I know she's wrong!

Albert became interested in math and physics. He studied a lot and became one of the greatest scientists the world has ever known. What a success! Albert Einstein was a brilliant man who never stopped asking questions!

▶ What did you read?

Circle the main idea.

a. Albert Einstein was a brilliant man.

b. Albert Einstein learned best by asking questions.

▶ Read again

Read these sentences. One word in each sentence is not correct. Find the word and cross it out. Write the correct word. Check your answers with a partner.

1. Miss Koch came into the classroom at exactly 8:30 this ~~evening~~. *morning*

2. We sat down on our soft, uncomfortable chairs.

3. Then we closed our thick books and began to study.

4. I was angry, but I spoke to her.

5. It was foggy and gray.

6. They all read the news.

▶ Show you understand

Look at the sentences from the reading. Mark (X) the words that describe Albert's feelings. Talk about your answers with a partner.

	How do you think Albert felt?			
	happy	sad	angry	frustrated
1. I had a question but Miss Koch said, "Not now."			X	X
2. She told me to write, "I will not talk in class" 50 times.				
3. I walked home alone.				
4. I love to listen to them talk about new inventions.				
5. My parents and their friends answer all my questions.				
6. My teacher thinks I will never be successful, but I know she's wrong!				

Think about these questions. Then discuss your ideas.

Albert Einstein

1. Why didn't the teacher let Albert ask a question?

2. Albert Einstein wrote, "Don't become a person of success, become a person of value."* What did he mean?

3. What did you like about school when you were a child? What didn't you like?

*value = importance or usefulness

 Turn to *Remember the Words* at the back of this book.

TALK ABOUT IT

A. Work in a small group. Study the information about *Make a Difference Day*. List the ways people will help other people.

On Make a Difference Day, People Help Other People

700 students and teachers will repair public schools.

2,000 children will bake bread for the elderly.

Teenagers will collect money to buy toys for needy children.

1,500 volunteers will clean parks.

Ways people will help people on *Make a Difference Day*
Volunteers will clean parks.

EXTRA! EXTRA! "Make a Difference Day" is a national day of helping others in the U.S. On the fourth Saturday of October, more than 1 million volunteers help people in their communities.

B. Think about these questions. Then ask and answer the questions with a partner.

> **1.** How can you make a difference? Name three ways you can help your family, your friends, or your community.
>
> **2.** "When we give, we get." Do you agree? Why or why not?

READ ABOUT IT

The Geraldi family has adopted 20 children.

Before You Read

Look at the picture and the caption. Look at the title of the reading. Guess the answers to the questions.

1. Why did the Geraldi family adopt 20 children?

   a. They love children.   **b.** The children needed their help.   **c.** a *and* b

2. How do they take care of so many children?

   a. They do it themselves.   **b.** They have help.

Read this magazine article. Think about your guesses while you read.

For the **Love** of Children

Camille and Mike Geraldi love children. It's a good thing they do because they have 22.

Mike and Camille met when they were working at the same hospital. Mike was a pediatrician and Camille was a nurse. After dating for two years, they got married. Soon they had two healthy daughters, Renae and Jaclyn. They bought a house with a pool and drove expensive cars, but they weren't happy. Camille said, "I don't enjoy my life. I need to help people." So they started to adopt babies and toddlers who are mentally and physically challenged.

Now the Geraldi family has 20 adopted children, so Camille is very busy. She must take care of all the children, but she has help. The Geraldis' teenagers, Renae and Jaclyn, like to be helpful. Also, three adult helpers come every day.

Camille and Mike get up at 5:00 a.m. to greet the helpers. Together they wake up, bathe, and dress the children. At about 6:00 a.m. Camille makes their breakfast. After breakfast two of the helpers take most of the children to school. At 7:30 a.m.

Mike goes to work and Camille takes a nap. She naps for two hours. When she wakes up, she begins the laundry. She does about 12 loads of laundry every day.

After lunch Camille is even busier. She and the children swim, exercise, and play. Then she gives some of them physical therapy. Twice a week Camille goes to the market. She buys a lot of food. She buys 8 gallons (29.5 liters) of milk and 50 jars of baby food each time. She usually spends more than $700 a week.

At 5:00 p.m. Camille cooks dinner. She sometimes cooks for 30 people a day. Mike comes home about 6:00 p.m., and they all have dinner together. After dinner Mike cleans up the kitchen, and Camille helps Renae and Jaclyn do their homework. Camille and Mike go to bed around midnight. Camille doesn't get much sleep because some of the children wake up during the night.

Mike and Camille are tired but happy. They are proud to take care of their large family, and they plan to adopt more children. Now Mike and Camille say they truly enjoy their lives. 🤍

▶ What did you read?

Circle the main idea.

a. The Geraldis' family is a lot of work.   **b.** Mike and Camille love to adopt children.

▶ Read again

A. Are these sentences true? Find the answers in the reading. Circle *yes* or *no*. Check your answers with a partner.

1. Camille and Mike love children.   (yes)   no

2. Camille and Mike met at work.   yes   no

3. They have a lot of children.   yes   no

4. It's easy to take care of the children.   yes   no

5. Camille doesn't cook much.   yes   no

6. Mike helps Camille at home.   yes   no

B. Write the clues from the reading that helped you answer questions 4, 5, and 6 above.

4. Camille is very busy... she has help...

5. _____

6. _____

▶ Show you understand

What does Camille do every day? Fill in the chart with information from the reading.

Camille's Daily Routine	
5:00 a.m.	
5:00–6:00 a.m.	wakes up, bathes, and dresses children
6:00–7:30 a.m.	
7:30–9:30 a.m.	
9:30 a.m.–noon	
noon–1:00 p.m.	makes and serves lunch
1:00–5:00 p.m.	
5:00–7:00 p.m.	
7:00–10:00 p.m.	
midnight	

Think about these questions. Then discuss your ideas.

> 1. Why did Mike and Camille adopt these children? Give as many reasons as you can.
>
> 2. How do you think Renae and Jaclyn feel about their large family?
>
> 3. Do you know anyone who adopted children? Why did they adopt?

After You Read

▶ *Words, words, words*

A. Read the sentences. What do the <u>underlined</u> words mean? Look for clues in the reading. Write the letters of the correct meanings in the blanks.

    a. pays   **d.** like

    b. make a part of the family   **e.** working hard

    ~~**c.**~~ physically and mentally well

  _C_   **1.** Soon they had two <u>healthy</u> daughters, Renae and Jaclyn.

_____ **2.** Camille said, "I don't <u>enjoy</u> my life."

_____ **3.** ...they plan to <u>adopt</u> more children.

_____ **4.** Camille is <u>busy</u> taking care of all the children.

_____ **5.** She usually <u>spends</u> about $700 a week.

B. Study this word family. Look at the examples. Then fill in the blanks with the correct words.

Word Family	Examples
help *verb*	...Camille *helps* Renae and Jaclyn do their homework.
helper *noun*	Also, three adult *helpers* come every day.
helpful *adjective*	...Renae and Jaclyn like to be *helpful*.

      Mike and Camille have three adult _____. They also _____ each other. Their daughters are _____, too.

► *Write*

Think about a time you helped someone. Write a paragraph about it on your own paper. Use the questions and the example to help you.

1. Who did you help?
2. What was the problem?
3. What did you do?

4. How did the person feel?
5. How did you feel?

> Last month I helped my friend Amanda. She had to go to the hospital, and she couldn't take her son to school. I took him to school in the morning. Then I picked him up in the afternoon and cooked dinner for him. My friend felt relieved. I felt sad that Amanda was sick, and I was glad I could help her.

READ MORE ABOUT IT

Before You Read

Look at the picture. Read the title and the first sentence of the reading. Guess the answers to the questions.

1. What is the relationship between the young women?

   a. They are sisters.   **b.** They are friends.   **c.** They are cousins.

2. One of the young women is working in the garden. Why isn't the other one working?

   a. She is sick.   **b.** She is tired.   **c.** She is lazy.

3. What are the young women going to do next?

   a. shop at the market   **b.** visit the palace   **c.** go swimming

4. Is this a true story?

   a. yes   **b.** no   **c.** maybe

Read The Test, Part 1. Think about your guesses while you read.

The Test, Part 1

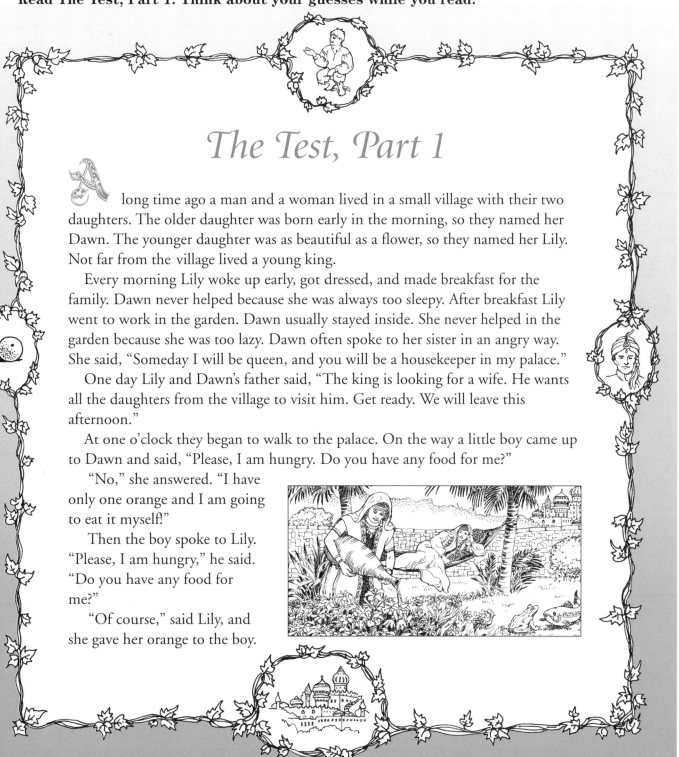

A long time ago a man and a woman lived in a small village with their two daughters. The older daughter was born early in the morning, so they named her Dawn. The younger daughter was as beautiful as a flower, so they named her Lily. Not far from the village lived a young king.

Every morning Lily woke up early, got dressed, and made breakfast for the family. Dawn never helped because she was always too sleepy. After breakfast Lily went to work in the garden. Dawn usually stayed inside. She never helped in the garden because she was too lazy. Dawn often spoke to her sister in an angry way. She said, "Someday I will be queen, and you will be a housekeeper in my palace."

One day Lily and Dawn's father said, "The king is looking for a wife. He wants all the daughters from the village to visit him. Get ready. We will leave this afternoon."

At one o'clock they began to walk to the palace. On the way a little boy came up to Dawn and said, "Please, I am hungry. Do you have any food for me?"

"No," she answered. "I have only one orange and I am going to eat it myself!"

Then the boy spoke to Lily. "Please, I am hungry," he said. "Do you have any food for me?"

"Of course," said Lily, and she gave her orange to the boy.

Are these sentences true? Find the answers in the reading. Circle *yes* or *no*. Check your answers with a partner.

1. Lily and Dawn are sisters.   (yes)   no

2. Lily and Dawn make breakfast together.   yes   no

3. The king wants a new worker.   yes   no

4. A young boy asks for food.   yes   no

5. Dawn is kind to him.   yes   no

6. Lily is kind to him.   yes   no

Before You Read

A. **Think about The Test, Part 1. Look at the guesses you made before you read it. Then answer these questions.**

1. Why didn't Dawn work in the garden? _____

2. What did the sisters do in the afternoon? _____

3. Is this a true story? How do you know? Give two reasons.

_____

_____

B. **Look at the pictures on page 17. Guess the answers to these questions.**

1. What's going to happen at the palace?

_____

2. Who's going to marry the king? How do you know?

_____

3. What's going to happen to the other sister?

_____

While You Read

Read The Test, Part 2. Think about your guesses while you read.

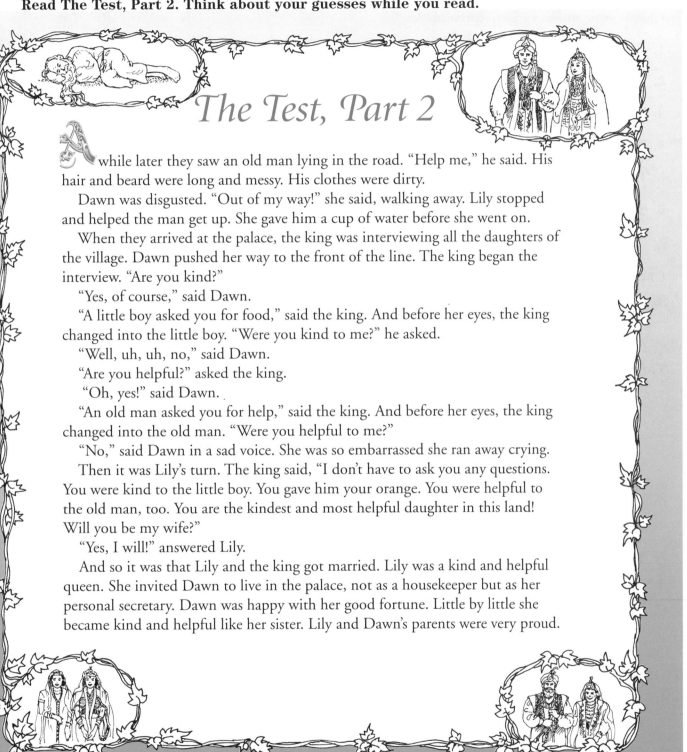

The Test, Part 2

A while later they saw an old man lying in the road. "Help me," he said. His hair and beard were long and messy. His clothes were dirty.

Dawn was disgusted. "Out of my way!" she said, walking away. Lily stopped and helped the man get up. She gave him a cup of water before she went on.

When they arrived at the palace, the king was interviewing all the daughters of the village. Dawn pushed her way to the front of the line. The king began the interview. "Are you kind?"

"Yes, of course," said Dawn.

"A little boy asked you for food," said the king. And before her eyes, the king changed into the little boy. "Were you kind to me?" he asked.

"Well, uh, uh, no," said Dawn.

"Are you helpful?" asked the king.

"Oh, yes!" said Dawn.

"An old man asked you for help," said the king. And before her eyes, the king changed into the old man. "Were you helpful to me?"

"No," said Dawn in a sad voice. She was so embarrassed she ran away crying.

Then it was Lily's turn. The king said, "I don't have to ask you any questions. You were kind to the little boy. You gave him your orange. You were helpful to the old man, too. You are the kindest and most helpful daughter in this land! Will you be my wife?"

"Yes, I will!" answered Lily.

And so it was that Lily and the king got married. Lily was a kind and helpful queen. She invited Dawn to live in the palace, not as a housekeeper but as her personal secretary. Dawn was happy with her good fortune. Little by little she became kind and helpful like her sister. Lily and Dawn's parents were very proud.

▶ *Read again*

**Complete the sentences below. Find the answers in the reading. Circle *a* or *b*.
Check your answers with a partner.**

1. When Dawn saw the old man she felt   **a.** happy.   **(b.)** disgusted.

2. Lily helped the man   **a.** get up.   **b.** lie down.

3. The king changed into   **a.** a boy.   **b.** a boy and an old man.

4. The king's questions made Dawn feel   **a.** tired.   **b.** embarrassed.

5. Lily and the king   **a.** got married.   **b.** went away.

6. The parents were proud because they had   **a.** kind daughters.   **b.** beautiful daughters.

▶ *What did you read?*

Choose another title for the reading. Circle the best one.

a. A Kind and Helpful Daughter   **b.** Two Sisters

▶ *Talk more about it*

Think about these questions. Then discuss your ideas.

1. How did the little boy and the old man feel when Lily helped them? How did Lily feel?

2. Why is this story called "The Test"?

3. A folktale often teaches us something about life. What does "The Test" teach us?

 Turn to *Remember the Words* at the back of this book.

TALK ABOUT IT

A. Work with a partner. Write the names of the rooms on this floor plan. Then ask and answer the questions with your partner.

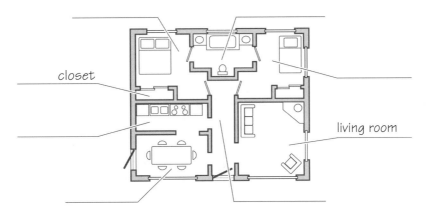

closet

living room

1. How many bedrooms does this house have? How many bathrooms?

2. Would you like to live in it? Why or why not?

3. Would you like to own this house? Why or why not?

B. Draw in the walls, windows, and closets on this floor plan. Label the rooms. Then ask and answer the questions with your partner.

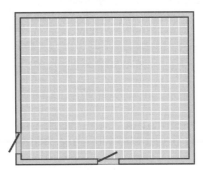

1. Did you design a house or an apartment? Why?

2. How many bedrooms does your house or apartment have? How many bathrooms? How many closets? Why?

Volunteers from the community are helping the Dean family build their house.

Before You Read

Look at the pictures and the captions. Look at the title of the reading. Guess which words and phrases will be in the reading. Mark (X) them.

_____ suburbs	_____ get a loan	_____ bedroom
_____ apartment	_____ pay the rent	_____ wash
_____ landlord	_____ floor plan	_____ carpenter
_____ move in	_____ backyard	_____ broom
_____ plumber	_____ sofa	_____ dining area

Read this newspaper article. Think about your guesses while you read.

PEOPLE

Hearts and Hands Build Homes

It's a sunny Saturday morning in North County. At 46 Elm Street, several people are standing next to a pile of lumber and bricks. They are going to build a house. But these people are not carpenters, plumbers, electricians, or roofers. They are students from a nearby high school and business people from the community. They are volunteers for Habitat for Humanity International, a group that helps build houses for low-income families all over the world. These volunteers give their time because they like to help people. Today they are going to help the Dean family build their new house.

The Deans can't wait until their house is finished. Now Kathy and Peter Dean and their three children are living in a two-bedroom apartment. Their landlord doesn't take care of the old building. "It is a terrible place! The walls are cracked, the roof leaks, and the furnace is always broken," Kathy said. "My family and I need a better place to live, but we don't have much money."

"We'll help the Deans pay for their new house," said a manager of Habitat for Humanity. "Peter and Kathy's home will cost about $35,000 to build. The family will get a loan from Habitat for Humanity, and they'll pay a mortgage of about $175 a month."

I can't believe we have a house! It's like a dream come true.

The Deans have to pay for their home and they also have to help build it. "We have to work 300 hours to build our own house," Peter said. "Then we have to work 300 more hours to help build another family's house," he added. "It's hard work, but it's worth it."

The Deans are excited about their new home. In about 1,000 square feet (90 square meters) of space, there will be three bedrooms, one bathroom, a living room, a kitchen, and a dining area. Kathy and Peter can't change the floor plan, but they can pick out the kitchen cabinets, floors, and light fixtures. After they move in, the Deans plan to build a fence and a garage. Kathy also wants to landscape the backyard. "I want to plant some bushes and flowers to make our yard beautiful," she said.

When the house is finished, the Deans will have a nice place to live and a large group of friends from the community. The Deans and the volunteers are working together to build something great. They are building a home and one family's future.

▶ What did you read?

Choose another title for this reading. Circle the best one.

a. A Community Builds for the Future   **b.** Build a House in 300 Hours

▶ Read again

Are these sentences true? Find the answers in the reading. Circle *yes* or *no*. Check your answers with a partner.

1. Habitat for Humanity helps build houses.	(yes)	no
2. Carpenters and electricians build the houses.	yes	no
3. Students and business people are volunteers.	yes	no
4. Now the Deans live in a nice apartment.	yes	no
5. The Deans have a lot of money.	yes	no
6. The Deans have to help build two houses.	yes	no
7. Their house will be 90 square feet.	yes	no

▶ Show you understand

Put these sentences in order. Number them from 1–7. Then retell the story to your partner. Add other details you remember.

_____ **a.** The Deans have to help build their house.

_____ **b.** So Habitat for Humanity is helping them build a house.

__1__ **c.** The Deans live in an apartment.

_____ **d.** Soon they will live in a three-bedroom house.

_____ **e.** The apartment has a lot of problems.

_____ **f.** Volunteers from the community work on it, too.

_____ **g.** They want a home of their own, but they don't have much money.

▶ Talk more about it

Think about these questions. Then discuss your ideas.

1. Why does Habitat for Humanity help people build homes?

2. Why does the Dean family have to help build their own home? Another family's home?

3. Do you ever volunteer? What do you do? Why?

After You Read

▶ *Pronouns*

The circled words are pronouns. What do they mean? Draw arrows to the words that tell the meanings.

1. At 46 Elm Street, several people are standing in front of a pile of lumber and bricks. (They) are going to build a house.

2. The volunteers give their time because (they) like to help people.

3. Their landlord doesn't take care of the old building. "(It) is a terrible place!"

4. "My family and I need a better place to live, but (we) don't have much money."

5. "We have to work 300 hours to build our own house," Peter said. "Then we have to help build another family's house," (he) added.

6. Kathy also wants to landscape the backyard. "I want to plant some bushes and flowers to make our yard beautiful," (she) said.

▶ *Words, words, words*

Read the sentences. What do the underlined words mean? Write the letters of the correct meanings in the blanks. Use clues in the reading to help you, and write the clues you find.

a. people who help others for free   **c.** in many countries in the world

b. plant grass, trees, bushes, and flowers   **d.** place where people live and work

Clues

__d__ 1. They are students from a nearby high school and business people from the community.   *nearby*

_____ 2. They are volunteers for Habitat for Humanity International...

_____ 3. The volunteers give their time because they like to help people.

_____ 4. Kathy also wants to landscape the backyard.

▶ *Write*

Write a paragraph about the Deans on your own paper. Use the questions and the model to help you.

1. Do the Deans like their apartment? Why or why not? Give three reasons.

2. Will the Deans like their house? Why or why not? Give three reasons.

    The Deans (like/don't like) their apartment because _____, _____, and

    _____. Soon they will move to a new house. They will (like/not like) it

    because _____, _____, and _____.

Before You Read

skim = read quickly to get the general idea
scan = look quickly to find specific information

**A. Look at the pictures. Skim the reading.
Circle the answer. What kind of reading is this?**

   1. a diary   **2.** a newspaper article   **3.** a brochure

B. Scan the reading for these numbers. Then draw a line to the matching words.

   1. 270   **a.** number of days to build in Japan

   2. 2   **b.** square feet in this home

   3. 6   **c.** price of a window box

   4. $399   **d.** number of friends needed to help

   5. $99   **e.** cost of shutters

While You Read

Read this selection. Check your answers while you read.

Everything you need in 270 square feet!

Hard to believe? Well, it's true. Ask architect Young-Jae Kim. He designed this beautiful home. It's small—only 15' x 18' (4.5 m x 5.4 m)—but it has everything you need.

Order your E-Z Home from the factory today!

We can deliver almost anywhere in the world. When you receive your E-Z Home, ask 2 friends to help you put it together. All you need is a screwdriver and a wrench.* In about a week you will have your own E-Z Home!

*You must hire an electrician and a plumber to hook up the electricity and water.

In the cozy living area you can put your feet up on a comfortable sofa and watch your favorite TV show. You can fit a dining room table and chairs in the dining area. The kitchen has a refrigerator, stove, oven, and microwave. A twin bed and a small dresser fit in the sleeping area. And the bathroom has a shower, sink, toilet, and medicine cabinet.

You even get a loft for storage or extra sleeping space. You can choose carpet for the floors and paint for the walls and ceilings. You can also order shutters, a window box, and a picket fence.

Do you need more space? The most exciting thing about this house is that it can grow with your needs. You can add a bedroom or a family room at any time.

Kobe, Japan:
In 1995 an earthquake destroyed my house, and I needed a new one quickly. This one took only 6 days to build. I am happy to be in my own home again.

Curitiba, Brazil:
I love my new home!

Vancouver, Canada:

I never wanted to live in a factory-built home. But when I looked at E-Z Homes, I was surprised. They are beautiful!

ORDER FORM

- ☐ E-Z Home 15' x 18' ·················· $15,999**
- ☐ Extra Bedroom 15' x 18' ············ $11,999
- ☐ Family Room 15' x 18' ··············· $11,999
- ☐ Shutters ····························· $399
- ☐ Picket Fence ························· $499
- ☐ Window Box ·························· $99

**Land and shipping costs not included in the total price

▶ What did you read?

The words below make a sentence about the main idea of the reading. Put them in the correct order and write the sentence on the line.

| need | all | ~~a~~ | be | house | can | small | you |

_____A_____ .

▶ Read again

Complete these sentences. Find the answers in the reading. Circle _a_ or _b_.

1. An E-Z Home is   **a.** 15 square feet.   (**b.**) 15' x 18'.
2. An E-Z Home is   **a.** easy to build.   **b.** difficult to build.
3. In the sleeping area you can put a   **a.** large dresser.   **b.** small dresser.
4. The kitchen comes with a   **a.** dishwasher.   **b.** microwave.
5. You can use the loft for   **a.** a dining area.   **b.** storage.
6. The house costs about the same as   **a.** a car.   **b.** most homes.

▶ Show you understand

Fill in the blanks with the words from the box.

| kitchen | space | build | dining | bedroom | screwdriver | ~~small~~ |

E-Z Home is _____small_____, but it has everything you need. It has a living area, a _____, a sleeping area, a _____ area, and a bathroom. All you need is a _____ and a wrench to put the house together, and you can _____ your house in about a week. When you need more _____, you can add a _____ or a family room.

▶ Talk more about it

Think about these questions. Then discuss your answers.

1. Who buys this kind of house? Why?
2. Would you like to live in this kind of house? Why or why not?

 Turn to _Remember the Words_ at the back of this book.

TALK ABOUT IT

A. Work with a partner. Read the cartoon. Then answer the questions.

1. Are Alexander and Cookie going to eat dinner at home? Why or why not?

_____

2. Do Blondie and Dagwood want to make a home-cooked meal? Why or why not?

_____

3. How do Blondie and Dagwood feel in the last picture? Why?

_____

4. In this cartoon, Blondie and Dagwood eat out at a restaurant. What else could they do for dinner?

_____

B. Think about these questions. Then ask and answer the questions with your partner.

1. In your country, do families usually eat meals together? Why or why not?

2. Who cooks the meals in your home?

3. Do you ever eat out? Where? Why?

Before You Read

Look at the pictures. Look at the title of the reading. Guess the answers to the questions.

1. What are these people doing?

_____

2. What do you think this reading is about?

    a. cooking meals   **b.** buying meals   **c.** planning meals

Read this magazine article. Think about your guesses while you read.

WHAT'S COOKING?

What's cooking? Nothing! Nothing's on the stove. Nothing's in the oven. Almost no one has time to cook anymore. Both women and men work. Parents are spending time with their kids. Senior citizens are out playing tennis or golf, and teenagers are always busy.

Everybody needs to eat, but meals need to be quick and easy! So what do we do? Nearly 80% of people in the United States buy take-out food at least once a month. Many people buy it every day. Most of us are in a hurry so we get fast food like pizza, hamburgers, or tacos. We often eat in our cars. But some of us are tired of eating fast food. We want to eat dinner at home with our families and friends. We want food that tastes like home cooking. We're hungry for healthy meals with main dishes like broiled fish, roast beef, or pasta and side dishes like rice, potatoes, or steamed vegetables. And sometimes we want dessert like cake, pie, or cookies. Fortunately, there are two new solutions to this problem: convenience stores and computers.

Many convenience stores are on street corners. Others are in shopping centers or in gas stations. People can get to these stores easily and shop quickly. Convenience stores usually sell beverages, snack foods, and milk. Many also sell packaged foods and produce.

Now some convenience stores are selling fresh, tasty meals that are ready to eat. Others are selling refrigerated foods that you can heat up quickly in the microwave oven at home.

Walk into a place like Michael's Market and you'll find healthy, fresh meals. On Mondays you can buy lasagna with garlic bread and fresh green salad. You can get cheese enchiladas with beans and rice on Tuesdays, and Thai barbecued chicken with stir-fried broccoli and mushrooms on Wednesdays. Try the daily special of roast chicken, carrots, and mashed potatoes. Take home freshly baked bread, blueberry pie, and chocolate chip cookies every day of the week.

There is another solution if you are too busy to cook your own dinner. Just use your computer to look up food businesses on the Internet. Webvan delivers groceries and prepared meals. Food.com will show you a list of restaurants in your neighborhood. You can also see the menus. Type the name of the restaurant and the meal you want on the Web page. Your dinner can be ready in an hour. You can also order dinner for next week or next month. The restaurant will deliver your meal to your home or business, or you can pick it up.

Now you don't need to cook to get a good, hot meal. All you need is a convenience store or your computer…and a good appetite!

▶ What did you read?

Circle the main idea.

a. A lot of people buy fast food and eat in their cars.

b. You don't have to cook to get fresh, tasty meals.

▶ Read again

A. Are these sentences true? Find the answers in the reading. Circle *yes* or *no*. Check your answers with a partner.

1. Most people have time to cook dinner.	yes	(no)
2. People buy take-out food because it's fast.	yes	no
3. Most people cook and eat a good, healthy meal.	yes	no
4. You can buy fresh, tasty meals at some convenience stores.	yes	no
5. It's fast and easy to buy a meal at a convenience store.	yes	no
6. You can save time when you order a meal by computer.	yes	no

B. Write the clues from the reading that helped you answer questions 2, 5, and 6 above.

2. Most of us are in a hurry...

5. _____

6. _____

▶ Show you understand

Describe these ways to get meals. Are they fast, easy, healthy, or tasty? Circle your answers. Talk about your answers with your partner.

1. Cook meals at home	fast	easy	(healthy)	(tasty)
2. Get fast food	fast	easy	healthy	tasty
3. Buy meals at a convenience store	fast	easy	healthy	tasty
4. Order meals by computer	fast	easy	healthy	tasty

▶ Talk more about it

Think about these questions. Then discuss your ideas.

> **1.** Many people do not cook because they are busy. How does that change their lives? Name three ways.
>
> **2.** Would you go to a convenience store or use a computer to buy meals? Why or why not?

After You Read

▶ *Words, words, words*

A. Read the sentences. What do the underlined words mean? Look for clues in the reading. Write the letters of the correct meanings in the blanks.

a. desire to eat	**c.** answers	~~**e.**~~ bored with	**g.** cold
b. food made at home	**d.** fast	**f.** good for you	

___e___ **1.** But some of us are <u>tired of</u> eating fast food.

_____ **2.** We want food that tastes like <u>home cooking</u>.

_____ **3.** We're hungry for <u>healthy</u> meals with a main dish like broiled fish...

_____ **4.** ...but meals need to be <u>quick</u> and easy!

_____ **5.** Fortunately, there are two new <u>solutions</u> to this problem.

_____ **6.** Others are selling <u>refrigerated</u> foods that can be heated up quickly in the microwave oven at home.

_____ **7.** All you need is a convenience store or your computer...and a good <u>appetite</u>!

B. Study this word family. Look at the examples. Then fill in the blanks with the correct words.

Word Family	Examples
quick *adjective* easy *adjective*	Everybody needs to eat, but meals need to be *quick* and *easy*.
easily *adverb* quickly *adverb*	People can get to these stores *easily* and shop *quickly*.

It's _____ to buy healthy meals at Michael's Market. You can buy delicious, fresh food there. And it's _____. You can get there _____ and buy your meal _____.

READ MORE ABOUT IT

Before You Read

Look at the pictures. Look at the reading and the title of the reading. Guess the answers to the questions. Circle them.

1. What kind of reading is this?

   a. a diary   **b.** a poem   **c.** a newspaper article

2. What is this reading about?

While You Read

Read this selection aloud. Think about your guesses while you read.

Knoxville, Tennessee

by Nikki Giovanni

I always like summer best
you can eat fresh corn
from daddy's garden
and okra
and cabbage
and lots of
barbecue
and buttermilk
and homemade ice-cream
at the church picnic

and listen to
gospel music
outside
at the church
homecoming
and go to the mountains with
your grandmother
and go barefooted
and be warm
all the time
not only when you go to bed
and sleep

► *What did you read?*

Circle the main idea.

a. An adult remembers the summer.

b. A child tells why she likes summer.

► *Read again*

What does the writer like? Fill in the chart with information from the reading.

What does she like to eat?	Where does she like to go?	What does she like to do?
fresh corn		

► *Talk more about it*

Think about these questions. Then discuss your ideas.

1. How does the writer feel about summer? Why?

2. Think about a food or meal from your childhood. What is it? Why did you like or not like it? Who made it for you? Where did you eat it? When did you eat it?

► *Write*

Write a poem about the season you like best on your own paper. Use the questions, the model, and Nikki Giovanni's poem to help you.

1. What season do you like best?

2. What foods do you like to eat in that season?

3. Where do you like to go in that season?

4. What do you like to do in that season?

I always like (1) _____ best

you can eat (2) _____

and (2) _____

and (2) _____

and go (3) _____

and (3) _____

and (4) _____

and (4) _____

 Turn to *Remember the Words* at the back of this book.

Fashion Statements

TALK ABOUT IT

A. Work with a partner. Look at the graph. Circle the correct answers.

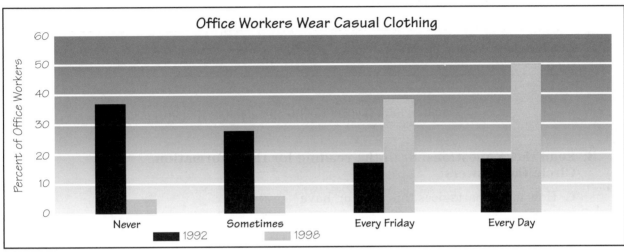

Based on information from the Society for Human Resource Management, Levi Strauss & Co., and *Daily News Record*. Percentages are approximate.

1. How many office workers wore casual clothing every day in 1992?   **a.** 19%   **b.** 50%

2. How many office workers never wore casual clothing in 1992?   **a.** 5%   **b.** 37%

3. How many office workers sometimes wore casual clothing in 1998?   **a.** 6%   **b.** 28%

4. How many office workers wore casual clothing every Friday in 1998?   **a.** 39%   **b.** 50%

5. More office workers wore casual clothing in 1998 than in 1992.   **a.** yes   **b.** no

B. Think about these questions. Then ask and answer the questions with your partner.

1. By 2015, how many office workers do you think will wear casual clothing every day? _____%

2. What do you usually wear to work or school?

3. When you choose clothes, what is most important? Why? Rate the following items from 1–7. Number 1 is most important.

_____ fashion   _____ comfort   _____ price

_____ color   _____ fit   _____ same as friends' clothes

_____ other _____

Before You Read

A. Look at the cartoon. Read the caption. Guess the answers to the questions.

1. Where are these men? What are they talking about?

_____

2. What does *grubby* mean?

_____

scan = look quickly to find specific information

B. Read these questions. Scan the reading for the information. Circle the answers.

1. How many parts does this reading have?

   a. 2   **b.** 4   **c.** 5

2. How many office workers wear casual clothing to work?

   a. 72.7 million   **b.** 95%

Dressing Down

It's "casual" Friday, Whitmore, not "grubby" Friday!

While You Read

Read this memo. Check your answers while you read.

RAAI, Inc.

MEMO

To: All Employees
From: Pablo Chavez, Director of Human Resources
Re: Casual Fridays

Casual Fridays are becoming popular at companies around the world. Should our company have Casual Fridays? Please fill out this questionnaire and return it to me by Wednesday. I am attaching a magazine article about Casual Fridays for your information.

Casual Friday Questionnaire

• Do you want to wear casual clothing to work on Fridays?

            yes   no   maybe

• Which clothing do you think people should wear on Casual Fridays? Circle your choices.

Men
1. casual pants
2. sports coats
3. sports shirts
4. ties

Women
5. pants
6. long dresses
7. leggings

Men or Women
8. jeans
9. tank tops
10. knit shirts
11. T-shirts
12. sweaters
13. sweatshirts/sweatpants

14. shorts
15. athletic shoes
16. sandals
17. other:

DressRight Magazine's
FACTS ABOUT CASUAL FRIDAYS

• Many large companies in Japan, Italy, France, Germany, and the United States allow office workers to wear casual clothing. Workers at companies like Honda Motor Company, United Airlines, and IBM can wear casual clothing every day of the week.

• There are 72.7 million office workers in the United States. Almost 95% of these workers wear casual clothing at least once a week, usually on Fridays. That's where the name "Casual Fridays" comes from.

• Wearing casual clothing is good for workers and employers. Casual clothing makes workers feel more comfortable at work. When workers are more comfortable, they work together better and get more work done. Workers also save money on buying and dry cleaning clothing.

Tips for Casual Days

	If you usually wear:	On casual days you can wear:
WOMEN	dresses or skirts with jackets	skirts or pants with cardigan sweaters or vests
	silk or polyester blouses	cotton knit shirts
MEN	suit or sports coat with dress slacks	casual pants; sports shirts, turtlenecks, or knit shirts with or without sports coats or sweaters
	ties	no ties

▶ *What did you read?*

The words below make a sentence about the main idea of the reading. Put them in the correct order and write the sentence on the line.

| wear | to | ~~Many~~ | casual | work | office workers | clothing |

Many _____ .

▶ *Read again*

Are these sentences true? Find the answers in the reading. Circle *yes* or *no*. Check your answers with a partner.

1. Casual Fridays are popular around the world.   (yes)   no

2. Workers should return the questionnaire on Friday.   yes   no

3. The questionnaire gives 20 choices of clothing.   yes   no

4. Casual clothing helps workers work harder.   yes   no

5. Casual clothing helps workers save money.   yes   no

6. On casual days men usually wear ties.   yes   no

7. On casual days women often wear pants.   yes   no

▶ *Show you understand*

Look at DressRight Magazine's "Tips for Casual Days" on page 37. Then look at the questionnaire. Which items of clothing should workers wear on Casual Fridays? Circle them. Discuss your answers with a partner.

▶ *Talk more about it*

Think about these questions. Then discuss your ideas.

1. In what year do you think Pablo Chavez wrote this memo? Give reasons for your answer.

2. Should workers wear casual clothing to work? Why or why not?

3. Should teachers wear casual clothing to school? Should students? Why or why not?

After You Read

▶ *Brainstorm and write*

Imagine that someone new has just come to your school, workplace, or community. What tips would you give that person about what to wear?

Brainstorm some ideas with a partner. Then use the chart to write a tip sheet. Share your tip sheet with the class and give reasons for your tips.

CLOTHING TIPS

Men should usually wear...	sometimes wear...	never wear...
Women should usually wear...	sometimes wear...	never wear...

Before You Read

Look at the picture. Read the caption. Look at the title of the reading. Guess the answers to the questions.

1. What does a coolhunter hunt?

   _____

2. What is this reading about?

   _____

While You Read

Read this interview. Think about your guesses while you read.

Coolhunters

Radio host Deborah Amos interviewed Baysie Wightman and Deedee Gordon. These two women are quickly becoming the coolest fashion designers of the 21st century. They call themselves coolhunters.

Deborah: Why do you call yourselves coolhunters? What are coolhunters?

Deedee: We hunt for cool kids. We look for kids who don't look or dress like everybody else. Somebody a little different. We look at what these kids are wearing and see how we can design an outfit everybody will like.

Baysie: You know, fashion designers used to start new fashions. For example, Calvin Klein helped make jeans fashionable. But today, it's different. Fashion comes from the streets.

A coolhunter finds fashion in New York.

Coolhunters Continued

Deborah: So how do you find the coolest kids?

Baysie: We go to big cities like Tokyo, New York, Seattle, London, or Los Angeles. We visit small clothing stores, not big department stores. Or we stand on the street. When we see kids we think are cool, we talk to them and take pictures of their clothes. Usually what the cool kid is wearing is what other people will want to wear 6 to 12 months from now.

Deborah: But how do you know what will be popular?

Deedee: It's just a feeling. For example, a few years ago I was in Los Angeles. I saw some kids wearing socks with sandals and I knew that idea would sell. We took that look, put a bigger sole on the sandal, and everyone loved it.

Deborah: Why were kids wearing socks with sandals?

Baysie: Who knows why? Fashion just happens. In Seattle all the kids wanted that "old man" look. You know, large, plaid shirts and polyester pants. And in Japan, girls were wearing short dresses with high-tech athletic shoes. I can't explain it.

Deedee: And now athletes are not the only ones wearing athletic clothes. Everyone is wearing them. You see people wearing leggings, bike shorts, sweatpants, and sweatshirts for every day. And people are wearing silk jogging suits to go to night clubs.

Deborah: How do you think that became fashionable?

Deedee: People love sports, and they love to wear casual clothes. So it's natural. Today people will never play sports in 80% of the athletic clothes they buy. They just like to wear them.

Deborah: So, Baysie, what will be the next cool fashion?

Baysie: I don't know, but I'm going to look for it right now!

▶*What did you read?*

The words below make a sentence about the main idea of the reading. Put them in the correct order and write the sentence on the line.

kids   cool   ~~Fashion~~   from   get   designers   ideas

Fashion _____.

▶ *Read again*

**Are these sentences true? Find the answers in the reading. Circle *yes* or *no*.
Check your answers with a partner.**

1. Coolhunters look for cool kids.   (yes)   no

2. The coolhunters are fashion designers.   yes   no

3. Cool kids look like everybody else.   yes   no

4. Designers start all new fashions.   yes   no

5. Coolhunters look for cool kids in big cities.   yes   no

6. Coolhunters find cool kids in department stores.   yes   no

7. People wear athletic clothes only to play sports.   yes   no

▶ *Show you understand*

Fill in the blanks with words from the box.

cool	clothing	~~hunt~~	street	find	pictures

Baysie and Deedee _____hunt_____ for cool kids. They find them in

small _____ stores or on the _____. Baysie and Deedee talk to

the kids and take _____ of their clothing. They want to _____

the next _____ fashion.

▶ *Talk more about it*

Think about these questions. Then discuss your ideas.

> 1. Why do coolhunters look for cool kids in big cities?
>
> 2. Why don't coolhunters look for cool kids in department stores?
>
> 3. Do you prefer to wear a new fashion when it first comes out or
>   wait until everyone is wearing it? Why?

 Turn to *Remember the Words* at the back of this book.

TALK ABOUT IT

A. Walk around the class. Ask each classmate a different question from the list below. When you find someone who answers *yes*, write his or her name in the blank. Get at least one name for each blank.

Do you…

1. …exercise every day? _____

2. …exercise 3 or more times a week? _____

3. …eat 5–9 servings of fruits or vegetables every day? _____

4. …get 8 hours of sleep every day? _____

5. …get acupuncture? _____

6. …go to a chiropractor? _____

7. …get regular checkups from a doctor? _____

8. …take time to relax every day? _____

B. Think about these questions. Then ask and answer the questions with a partner.

> **1.** How do you stay healthy? Name three things you do.
>
> **2.** What do you do when you get a cold? The flu? An infection?

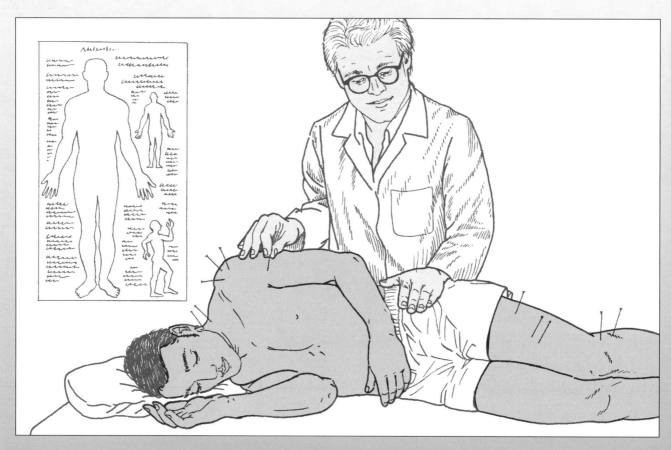

How can needles make this man feel better?

Before You Read

Look at the picture and the caption. Look at the title of the reading. Guess the answers to the questions.

1. Where is this man?

   _____

2. What's happening to him?

   _____

Read this newspaper article. Think about your guesses while you read.

No More Pain

Daniel DaSilva is lying on a table. A dozen thin needles are sticking out of his back, shoulders, arms, legs, and neck. He looks like a human pincushion, but he doesn't care. Daniel is getting an acupuncture treatment, and the needles make him feel better.

After the treatment Daniel talked about his experience with acupuncture. "A year ago I had a car accident, and I was in a lot of pain," said Daniel. "My doctor gave me prescription medication, and I had physical therapy. That made me feel a little better, but I was still in pain. Then my doctor sent me to get acupuncture. I was scared at first. I thought the needles would hurt, but they didn't. In the beginning the treatment didn't seem to help. But now my pain is almost gone."

Before every treatment the acupuncturist examines Daniel and asks about his physical symptoms. He also looks at what Daniel eats. He studies Daniel's thoughts and feelings, too. Then the acupuncturist treats the pain by putting thin needles into specific points on Daniel's body.

In China people have used acupuncture for thousands of years. It has been common in Korea and in Japan for centuries. Since the 1980s acupuncture has become popular in Europe, Canada, and the United States. At first many doctors in these parts of the world were not sure acupuncture really helped people. So they studied acupuncture for many years. They began to see that the treatments often helped their patients.

In 1997 the U.S. National Institutes of Health wrote a report about acupuncture. The report said that acupuncture stops some kinds of nausea and pain. It also said that acupuncture helps headaches and asthma. Some people believe it is an excellent treatment for allergies and arthritis. Acupuncturists also treat athletes for muscle soreness and injuries.

Now medical schools in the United States are teaching doctors about acupuncture. More than 4,000 medical doctors use acupuncture in their offices. Some doctors, like Daniel's, are sending their patients to one of the 15,000 acupuncturists in the country. More and more health insurance companies are paying for acupuncture treatments.

Acupuncture is helping people. Research shows that it works. Soon it will be very common all over the world to see a human pincushion.

▶ *What did you read?*

Choose another title for this reading. Circle the best one.

a. Acupuncture Helps Headaches

b. All About Acupuncture

▶ *Read again*

**Complete these sentences. Find the answers in the reading. Circle *a* or *b*.
Check your answers with a partner.**

1. Daniel DaSilva had a (**a.**) car accident. **b.** headache.

2. He gets **a.** chiropractic treatments. **b.** acupuncture treatments.

3. Now Daniel feels **a.** much better. **b.** a little better.

4. His acupuncturist uses **a.** medication. **b.** needles.

5. In Europe acupuncture
   became popular **a.** in the 1980s. **b.** in the 1990s.

6. Athletes get acupuncture to treat **a.** illnesses. **b.** injuries.

▶ *Show you understand*

**Read these sentences. Fill in the chart and write the clues from the reading
that helped you choose your answers. Talk about your answers with your partner.**

	Yes	No	Clues
1. Daniel DaSilva thinks physical therapy helped him.	X		*That made me feel a little better...*
2. He thinks acupuncture helped him.			
3. Acupuncturists only look at the patient's physical symptoms.			
4. Acupuncture began in Japan.			
5. Many medical doctors believe acupuncture helps people.			
6. Some insurance companies believe acupuncture helps people.			

▶ *Talk more about it*

Think about these questions. Then discuss your ideas.

1. Is acupuncture popular in your country? Why or why not?

2. Would you get acupuncture treatments? Why or why not?

After You Read

▶ *Words, words, words*

A. Read the sentences. What do the <u>underlined</u> words mean? Look for clues in the reading. Write the letters of the correct meanings in the blanks.

    a. something you do to get better   **d.** place to keep pins

    b. person who gives acupuncture treatments   **e.** liked or done by a lot of people

    ~~**c.**~~ man, woman, or child

   _C_ **1.** He looks like a <u>human</u> pincushion…

   _____ **2.** He looks like a human <u>pincushion</u>…

   _____ **3.** Daniel is getting an acupuncture <u>treatment</u>…

   _____ **4.** Before every treatment, Daniel's <u>acupuncturist</u> examines his physical symptoms.

   _____ **5.** Since the 1980s acupuncture has become <u>popular</u> in Europe, Canada, and the United States.

B. Study this word family. Look at the examples. Then fill in the blanks with the correct words.

Word Family	Examples
treat *verb*	Acupuncturists also *treat* athletes for muscle soreness and injuries.
treatment *noun*	Some people believe it is an excellent *treatment* for allergies and arthritis.

    Acupuncture has become very popular. Acupuncturists _____ people for pain and illnesses. Studies show that the _____ works.

▶ *Write*

Have you ever had an accident or an illness? Write a paragraph about it on your own paper. Use the questions and the example to help you. Add some extra details.

1. What happened? When?   **3.** What were your physical symptoms?

2. How did you feel?   **4.** What did you do to get better?

    Last winter I got strep throat. I felt terrible. I had a high fever, and my throat was very sore. I went to the medical clinic, and my doctor gave me prescription medication. I took my medication and stayed in bed for three days. Then I went back to work.

Before You Read

Look at the picture and the words in the picture. Look at the title of the reading. Guess the answers to the questions.

1. People sometimes say, "An apple a day keeps the doctor away." What does this mean?

   _____

2. What is this reading about?

   _____

While You Read

Read this magazine article. Think about your guesses while you read.

An Apple a Day

"An apple a day keeps the doctor away!" But what about a carrot or a strawberry? For years doctors and dieticians have told us to eat more fruits and vegetables. Now they think fruits and vegetables may even prevent disease. Eating foods like grapes, corn, and spinach may keep us from getting sick.

How many fruits and vegetables should we eat? Experts say five to nine servings each day will keep us healthy. This may sound like a lot. Some people in the United States eat only one serving a day. But people from Asian and Mediterranean countries eat many servings of fruits and vegetables. In these countries, fewer people get cancer or heart disease than in the United States.

Here are some of the things doctors and dieticians have learned about fruits and vegetables:
- Eating a diet full of all kinds of fruits and vegetables may cut our chances of getting lung and colon cancer by 30–40%. It may also cut our chances of getting stomach cancer by 60%.
- Women who eat lots of brightly colored vegetables like carrots, spinach, tomatoes, and corn may cut their chances of getting breast cancer by 30–70%. Brightly colored fruits and vegetables have certain chemicals that fight diseases. Brighter colors mean more of these good chemicals.
- Spinach and yellow corn may prevent heart disease.
- Cranberry juice may prevent bladder infections. Women who take cranberry capsules get 40% fewer bladder infections.
- Grapes help fight allergies, heart attacks, and strokes.
- Soybeans may prevent osteoporosis, a disease of the bones. They may also prevent breast cancer. Eating only one serving of soybeans a week may cut the chances of getting breast cancer by 15%.
- Garlic may keep us healthy and may prevent colds, flu, and even cancer.

How can we remember which fruits and vegetables to eat? One dietician says, "Eat a colorful diet to stay healthy. Every day eat something orange like a mango, something yellow like a peach, something green like broccoli, and something red like tomatoes." If we follow this advice, we may be able to stay healthy and live longer.

FIGHT DISEASE

EAT FRUIT AND VEGETABLES

1 serving = 1/2 banana, 1 small apple, or 1/2 cup peas

▶ *What did you read?*

Circle the main idea.

a. Fruits and vegetables are important for good health.   **b.** People should eat apples every day.

▶ *Read again*

Look at the chart. Write the disease next to the food that may prevent it. Find the answers in the reading. You can write some diseases in more than one space.

Food	May help prevent...	Disease
all kinds of fruits and vegetables		lung, colon, and stomach cancer
spinach		
yellow corn		
grapes		
garlic		
soybeans		
cranberry juice		

Texas A & M University is trying to produce superveggies, which will have more of the chemicals that fight disease. For example, people will be able to eat one half of a supercarrot and get the same amount of good chemicals that are in three regular carrots.

▶ *Words, words, words*

Which words go together? Draw lines to match them.

1. fight ——————— heart disease, strokes, osteoporosis

2. cancer ⟍ prevent, cut the chances of getting

3. corn   oranges, grapes, mangoes, watermelon

4. apples   yellow, green, orange

5. red   spinach, broccoli, garlic

▶ *Talk more about it*

Think about these questions. Then discuss your ideas.

1. How many servings of fruits and vegetables do you think the average person eats in your country?

2. Do you eat 5–9 servings of fruits and vegetables every day? Why or why not? Give three reasons.

3. Do you eat colorful food? Name a red, yellow, green, and orange fruit or vegetable you like to eat.

 Turn to *Remember the Words* at the back of this book.

TALK ABOUT IT

A. Work with a partner. Match the newspaper headlines with the stories. Write the letters in the blanks.

_____ 1.
Drought Kills Crops

_____ 3.
Tornado Disaster

_____ 2.
Blizzard Closes City

_____ 4.
El Niño Brings Storms

a. More than five inches of rain fell last night and knocked down hundreds of power lines in the northern·part of the state.

b. Farmers are losing millions of dollars as dry, hot weather continues.

c. Heavy snow hit this morning and caused schools and businesses to shut down.

d. A twister with wind speeds of 210 mph (336 km/h) destroyed hundreds of houses.

B. Work with your partner. Check the correct boxes in the chart. Then discuss your answers with another pair of students. Tell why you chose your answers.

What should you do in these emergencies?	1. Mudslide Blocks Roads	2. City Loses Power	3. Storm Floods Town
Listen to the radio			
Use flashlights			
Keep refrigerator closed			
Use other roads			
Build a fire			
Move things off the floor			
Contact family members			
Fill containers with clean drinking water			

Before You Read

Look at the pictures and the captions. Look at the title of the reading. Guess the answers to the questions.

1. What is this reading about?

_____

2. What is the problem in the picture on page 53? What can the women do about it?

_____

While You Read

Read this magazine article. Think about your guesses while you read.

Friends in Need

Icy tree branches fell on power lines. Most of Montreal lost power.

Marie Dupont woke up suddenly. She heard a loud noise. She thought it was a gunshot, but it wasn't. It was the sound of a falling tree branch. Many branches were heavy with ice from a storm. The icy branches were cracking and falling onto power lines, homes, and cars.

It was a terrible storm. On January 5, 1998, freezing rain began to fall on parts of Canada and the United States. In five days, eight inches (20.32 cm) of freezing rain fell. Two million Canadians and more than half a million Americans lost electrical power. They did not have heat, and many people could not use their refrigerators or stoves. Some people did not have power for 15 days.

Southern Quebec and New England were at the center of the storm. Montreal, Canada, had the most problems. There were no lights in the downtown area because the power was out. Most stores and businesses were closed. All of the schools were closed. The downtown post office was closed, and letter carriers could not deliver the mail for several days. Travel was difficult. Sidewalks and streets were covered with ice. Traffic lights didn't work, and the subway stopped. People rushed to markets to buy food and emergency supplies. But some people had no money to buy things. They couldn't withdraw cash because the banks were closed and the ATMs were out of order.

During the emergency people called fire stations for help. Firefighters received six times more telephone calls than usual. The army also helped. Soldiers moved people into shelters, gave medical care, and cleaned up the tree branches and power lines.

Many people helped others. One hotel in Montreal let people stay there for half price. It also used two of its ballrooms as childcare

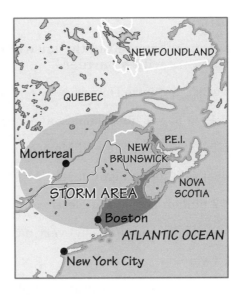

centers. A health club let people take hot showers. Families with power or supplies invited needy neighbors to stay with them.

During the storm people worked together to solve their problems. Marie Dupont left her house and was driving south. She had to stop because a tree was blocking the road. Another woman was driving north and stopped on the other side of the tree. They tried to move the tree but they couldn't. Then they had a great idea. Each woman climbed over the tree, borrowed the other woman's car, and went on her way.

People will remember the storm of 1998 for a long time. They will remember the many cold days with no heat. They will talk about the loud sounds of the breaking tree branches. And they will never forget how people helped each other during the worst storm of the 20th century. ■

▶ What did you read?

Choose another title for this reading. Circle the best one.

a. Emergency in Canada   **b.** The Storm of the Century

▶ Read again

**Are these sentences true? Find the answers in the reading. Circle *yes* or *no*.
Check your answers with a partner.**

1. A gunshot woke up Marie Dupont.	yes	(no)
2. Branches fell on power lines, homes, and cars.	yes	no
3. Freezing rain fell on Canada and Mexico.	yes	no
4. Five inches of rain fell in eight days.	yes	no
5. More than 2 million people lost electrical power.	yes	no
6. Letter carriers delivered the mail every day.	yes	no
7. Firefighters were busy.	yes	no
8. Some people shared their power and supplies.	yes	no
9. People will forget the storm soon.	yes	no

▶ Show you understand

Work with your partner. Fill in the chart with information from the reading.

During the storm...		
What was closed?	**What stayed open?**	**Who helped others?**
schools		

▶ Talk more about it

Think about these questions. Then discuss your ideas.

> 1. How did people cook their food when the power was out? How did they stay warm? Give three ideas.
>
> 2. Imagine your neighbors' home loses power. How could you help them? Name three ways.

After You Read

▶ *Words, words, words*

A. Match the words or phrases that have a similar meaning. Draw lines from the numbers to the correct letters.

1. power was out   **a.** sound
2. closed   **b.** shut down
3. stopped working   **c.** lost power
4. noise   **d.** out of order
5. money   **e.** shelter
6. home   **f.** cash

B. Study this word family. Look at the examples. Then fill in the blanks with the correct words.

Word Family	Examples
ice *noun*	Sidewalks and streets were covered with *ice*.
icy *adjective*	The *icy* branches cracked.

During the storm the _____ streets made travel difficult. The
_____ on the trees was heavy and made the branches crack.

▶ *Brainstorm and write*

Imagine the power is out in your city or town. What can you do? What can't you do? First work with a group to brainstorm answers to the questions in the chart. Then write as many sentences as you can that contrast your ideas. Follow the example.

The power is out... What can you do?	What can't you do?
go to the market	go to school

Example:

I can go to the market, but I can't go to school.

_____ but _____

_____ but _____

Before You Read

Look at the pictures and the caption. Look at the title of the reading. Guess the answers to the questions.

1. In this reading El Niño is

   a. a boy.   **b.** warm water in the Pacific Ocean.

2. What does El Niño cause?

   _____

While You Read

Read this newspaper article. Check your guesses while you read.

El Niño

In the 19th century, fishermen in Peru noticed something unusual. They saw that the Pacific Ocean water was sometimes warm in December. The fishermen called this *El Niño*. The warm water caused problems. It kept many fish away. The fishermen caught fewer fish, and their families were hungry.

Today El Niño still causes problems. Every two to seven years, warm water off Australia's coast moves east to South America. This changes the weather around the world. El Niño sometimes causes hot, dry weather in Southeast Asia, parts of South America, and Australia. It can also cause very heavy storms and high tides in eastern Africa and on the western coasts of North America, Central America, and South America.

El Niño made 1998 a difficult year. Parts of Canada and the United States lost power for 15 days because of an ice storm.

Look at what El Niño can do!

In Colorado a blizzard knocked down 31 square miles (80.6 square km) of trees. El Niño caused droughts in Indonesia, the Philippines, and Brazil. It brought tornadoes to Florida and New Mexico, mudslides to Peru and California, and floods to China, Somalia, and Ecuador. El Niño also brought some surprises. It caused warm winter weather in western Canada and fewer hurricanes in the Atlantic. It also brought snow to Guadalajara, Mexico, for the first time in more than 100 years.

Scientists are not sure what causes El Niño, but they agree that El Niño causes certain kinds of weather. This information is very helpful. For example, scientists can tell governments to plan for heavy rains. Then governments can protect public buildings such as city halls, schools, libraries, and courthouses from floods. Fire and police departments can plan how they will work together in case of emergency.

Scientists can also tell surfers where to find big waves. In March 1998 there was a surfing competition at Todos Santos, Mexico. Scientists said the waves would be big because of El Niño, and they were right. They were the

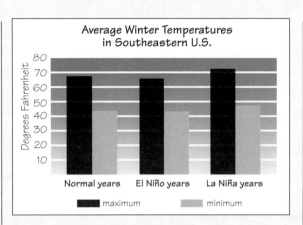

biggest waves ever surfed on the West Coast of North America! Some of the waves were more than 50 feet high (15.1 m). Taylor Knox won $50,000 for surfing a 52-foot wave.

Mark Twain said, "Everybody talks about the weather, but nobody does anything about it." Now scientists are doing something. They can't change the weather, but they can tell us more about it. Then we can be ready to protect our homes and communities and get ready for the big El Niño waves.

> **La Niña is the opposite of El Niño.**
> **Both La Niña and El Niño cause changes**
> **in winter weather around the world.**

▶ *What did you read?*

Circle the main idea.

a. El Niño causes hot, dry weather in Asia, South America, and Australia.

b. El Niño changes the weather around the world.

▶ *Read again*

Are these sentences true? Find the answers in the reading. Circle *yes* or *no*. Check your answers with a partner.

1. Indonesian fishermen gave El Niño its name.   yes   (no)

2. Warm water off Australia's coast moves west.   yes   no

3. In 1998 El Niño caused heavy rains in Brazil.   yes   no

4. Surfers like El Niño.   yes   no

5. Scientists can now change the weather.   yes   no

6. El Niño will cause problems in the future.   yes   no

7. La Niña makes the weather warmer than normal in some places.   yes   no

▶ *Show you understand*

What kinds of weather or natural disasters can El Niño cause? Find the answers in the reading and write them in the chart. Some countries may have more than one answer.

Brazil	drought	Mexico	
Canada		Peru	
China		Philippines	
Ecuador		Somalia	
Indonesia		United States	

▶ *Talk more about it*

Think about these questions. Then discuss your ideas.

1. How did people feel about the El Niño in 1998?

2. When was the last bad weather you remember? Talk about it.

3. How do El Niño and La Niña change the weather in your country?

 Turn to *Remember the Words* at the back of this book.

TALK ABOUT IT

A. Write one kind of transportation you have used in each of the circles. On the lines, write the places you have gone using that kind of transportation.

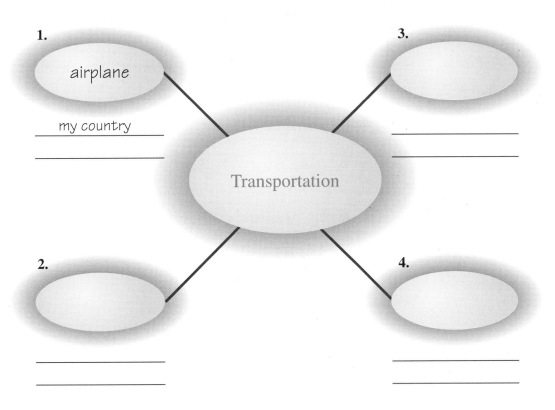

1. airplane

my country

3.

2.

4.

Transportation

B. Talk with a partner about the different kinds of transportation you have used and the places you have gone.

C. Think about these questions. Then ask and answer the questions with your partner.

> **1.** What is your favorite way to travel? Why?
>
> **2.** What is one kind of transportation you don't like? Why?

Before You Read

> skim = read quickly to get the general idea
> scan = look quickly to find specific information

A. Look at the pictures. Skim readings 1, 2, and 3. Circle the answer. What kind of readings are these?

   1. pages from a diary   **2.** newspaper articles   **3.** letters

B. Scan the readings. Write the answers in the blanks.

	Reading 1	Reading 2	Reading 3
1. What is the date of each one?	_____	_____	_____
2. What is the writer's name?	_____	_____	_____

While You Read

Read these selections. Check your answers while you read.

Traveling Through Time

Reading 1

San Francisco, California
July 28, 1925

Dear Essie,

   It was nice to meet you at Sandy's party. I was glad to give you a ride home. I am happy we are getting to know each other better.

   Right now I am waiting on the platform for a train and writing you this letter. I'm taking a business trip to Los Angeles. The trip is 425 miles (680 km) long, and it will take about 14 hours. I got a ticket for the last sleeper car, so at least I will have a bed to sleep in.

   My sister, Alice, lives in Los Angeles, so I will stay with her. I arrive at 7 a.m. Alice is going to meet me at the train station and drive me to her house. She just learned how to drive a few months ago and bought a new car for $500. I can't wait to see it. She is the first one of her friends to buy a car.

   I hope to see you when I return from my trip. May I take you out to dinner on the 10th?

Yours truly,
William

Reading 2

San Francisco, California
July 28, 1975

Dear Patti,

I'm sorry I had to cancel our lunch date today. What a day! I got to work at 8 a.m. and there was a message from our office in Los Angeles. They wanted me there by noon for a business lunch.

Luckily my office is near a subway station, so I took the subway to the airport. I got to the airline terminal at 8:45 and checked in. I boarded the plane at 8:55 and it took off on time. It was a direct flight, so I arrived in L.A. about an hour later. When my father traveled from San Francisco to Los Angeles in the 1920s, it took 14 hours by train!

At the airport I got into a taxi. When we got onto the highway, the traffic was stopped. You could see the brake lights for miles. There were just too many cars and trucks on the road. We finally got off the highway and drove on city streets. At the first stop sign, the driver made a left turn instead of a right turn and we got lost. It took us more than an hour to get to the office. The flight from San Francisco to Los Angeles took less time than that! Fortunately, I was on time for my meeting.

How about lunch next Tuesday? I'll take you to your favorite restaurant.

Yours,
Bill

Reading 3

To:	Eric@wol.com
From:	Willa@wol.com
Subject:	Hi!
Date:	July 28, 2025

Hi Eric,

I liked that movie we saw last week. It was fun to be with you.

I'm in Los Angeles for my weekly business meeting. I usually take the high-speed train from San Francisco to L.A. because it's so fast! My grandfather would be surprised. The train he rode in 1925 took 14 hours. Now the high-speed train takes only $1\frac{1}{2}$ hours!

Today I drove because I wanted to try the new automated highway. Have you tried it yet? It uses computers to connect the cars and the highway. It took $5\frac{1}{2}$ hours, but it was great. I turned on the computer in my sports car and got onto the highway. When I heard the beep, I slowly let go of the steering wheel. Then I took my foot off the gas pedal. My "smart" car drove, and I took a nap in the backseat. Can you believe it? The alarm clock woke me up before I arrived in L.A., and I told the computer the name of the off ramp. When I got close, the computer beeped. I put my hands on the steering wheel again and got off the highway. I drove straight to my meeting and got there at exactly 1:00.

Let's have dinner when I get back to San Francisco, OK?

See you soon.

Willa

Companies are testing automated highways now. By the year 2010 governments could start to build them.

▶ What did you read?

Circle the main idea.

a. Traveling is fun.   **b.** Transportation is always changing.

▶ Read again

Read these questions. Find the answers in the readings. Write them in the chart. Check your answers with a partner.

	Reading 1 1925	Reading 2 1975	Reading 3 2025
1. What kinds of transportation did the writer use?	train		
2. How long did it take the writer to get to Los Angeles?			
3. What time did the writer arrive in L.A.?			
4. Why did the writer go to L.A.?			

▶ Show you understand

Fill in the blanks with words from the box.

trips	grandfather	invite	~~friends~~	father	apologize

William, Bill, and Willa wrote letters to their ___friends___ . They

wanted to _____ them out to eat. They also wanted to tell them

about their _____ to Los Angeles. Bill also needed

to _____ to his friend because he cancelled their lunch date.

The three writers are in the same family. William is Bill's _____

and Willa's _____ .

▶ *Talk more about it*

Think about these questions. Then discuss your ideas.

> 1. Did William think it was a long trip from San Francisco to Los Angeles? Why or why not? How about Bill? How about Willa?
>
> 2. How did transportation change between 1925 and 1975? Between 1975 and now? How will it change by 2025?
>
> 3. What are some ways an automated highway will help drivers and communities?

After You Read

▶ *Find the reason*

Complete each sentence with the correct reason. Write the letters of your answers in the blanks.

1. __C__ William stayed with his sister

2. ____ William needed a ticket for the sleeper car

3. ____ Bill could see the brake lights

4. ____ It took an hour for Bill to get from the L.A. airport to the office

5. ____ Willa took her hands off the steering wheel

6. ____ The computer beeped

a. because traffic was stopped.

b. because her "smart" car was driving.

c. because she lived in Los Angeles.

d. because Willa's car was near the off ramp.

e. because the taxi driver got lost.

f. because the trip took a long time.

▶ *Write*

How would you like to get to work or school? Imagine you can build your own dream machine. Draw a picture of it. Now write a paragraph about the machine on your own paper. Tell why you want to build it and describe it. Use the example to help you.

I want to go to work in a flying car. I like to drive, but I hate traffic. My car will have wings so I can fly over the traffic. This car will be very fast. Then I can get to work on time.

Before You Read

Look at the pictures. Look at the title of the reading. Guess the answers to the questions.

1. What are these people doing?

_____

2. What does the title mean?

_____

While You Read

Read this magazine article. Think about your guesses while you read.

Get Out of Your Car!

Every day 100 million people in the United States get into their cars and drive to work alone. They sit in their cars on crowded roads, moving slowly. They look at all the other people alone in their cars, too. There has to be a better way to get to work!

There is! Some people take the bus or subway to work. Other people drive with friends in a car pool. Some companies buy vans so their workers can drive to work together.

Other companies are moving their offices to the suburbs so that more employees can walk to work. These are all good ideas, but some people are trying more unusual ways to get to work.

Garrett Jackson owns an athletic shoe store. To get to work he had to drive around the Santa Monica Mountains. He got home so late that he didn't have time for his hobby, running. Garrett likes to run marathons, races that are 26.2 miles (41.92 km) long. One day Garrett had an idea. He had to drive 15 miles around the mountain to get to his store, but it was only 7 miles over the mountain. So Garrett started running to work. Now Garrett enjoys his hobby twice a day.

Midori Harada was frustrated. Cars on Interstate 95 hadn't moved an inch for 15 minutes. She was going to be late for work, and she didn't know what to do. Then she remembered she had her daughter's inline skates in the trunk. Midori pulled off the highway and parked her car. She put on the skates, put her shoes in her briefcase, and skated to work. Now she skates to work almost every day. She gets to work faster and gets her exercise, too.

High in the Rocky Mountains, some people ski to work. The ski lift opens at 6 a.m. and takes these workers up the mountain. They ski down the other side to get to their jobs in town. At the end of the day, they put their skis on a bus and ride back home.

There are many ways to get out of our cars. There are many good reasons, too. If we leave our cars at home just one day a week, the air pollution in our cities will be 50% less. We will breathe more easily, get some exercise, and have some fun. ●

▶ *What did you read?*

Circle the main idea.

a. There are many different ways to get to work.

b. More people should leave their cars at home.

▶ *Read again*

Are these sentences true? Find the answers in the reading. Circle *yes* or *no*. Check your answers with a partner.

1. There are few cars on U.S. roads.   yes   (no)

2. Some companies help workers get out of their cars.   yes   no

3. Some people get exercise on their way to work.   yes   no

4. Garrett Jackson runs 26.2 miles to work every day.   yes   no

5. Midori Harada skates to work every day.   yes   no

6. Some people ski to work.   yes   no

7. There is more air pollution when people drive.   yes   no

▶ *Talk more about it*

Think about these questions. Then discuss your ideas.

1. Why is it important for people to leave their cars at home? Give three reasons.

2. How do most people get to work or school in your country? What are some unusual ways?

 Turn to *Remember the Words* at the back of this book.

TALK ABOUT IT

A. Work with a partner. Read this riddle. Try to guess the answer. Then check your answer with another pair of students.

Solve this Riddle

A boy needs an operation. A famous doctor walks into the operating room and says, " I cannot operate on this boy. He is my son." The doctor is not the boy's father.

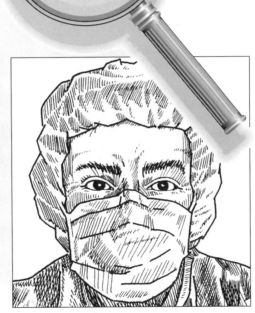

Who is the doctor?

B. Look at the answer to the riddle on page 113. Think about these questions. Then ask and answer the questions with a new partner.

1. Did you get the right answer to the riddle? Why or why not?

2. In your country, do men and women have different jobs? What are some men's jobs? What are some women's jobs?

3. Should men and women get equal pay for equal work?

Before You Read

A. Look at the pictures and the captions. Look at the title of the reading. Guess the answer to the question.

What is this reading about?

_____

B. Scan the reading for dates. Circle all the dates you find.

scan = look quickly to find specific information

1776   1820   1830   1860   1861   1900   1920   1945   1949   1981

Elizabeth Cady Stanton and
Susan B. Anthony led the
women's rights movement.

Read this page from a history book. Check your answers while you read.

A Woman's Place

The Declaration of Independence says, "All men are created equal." But women were not equal in 1776 when the United States became a country. A husband owned his wife. He also owned their children, their house, and everything in it. Women did not have those same rights. They could not own a house. They did not have the right to vote. At that time most people thought, "A woman's place is in the home."

Things changed slowly for women, but they *did* change. In the 1830s women started groups to fight for their rights. Lucretia Mott and Elizabeth Cady Stanton led the fight. Women wanted the right to own their homes, and they wanted the right to vote. In 1860 women won their first victory. A few states passed laws that gave married women the right to own houses. But women still couldn't vote.

In 1861 the Civil War began. The war took men away from their families, so many women had to do men's jobs for the first time. Some women were managers of farms or businesses. Some worked in factories and government offices. Women had no time to fight for their rights.

Sojourner Truth

After the war, women again began to work for the right to vote. Susan B. Anthony joined Mott and Stanton as a leader of the women's rights movement. Sojourner Truth, a freed slave, often gave speeches. But there was little change until World War I.

During World War I, women took men's jobs again, and many women worked in factories. There they made guns and other things used in the war. Their work helped the United States win the war, so President Wilson decided to help women win the right to vote. He worked to change the law to allow women to vote and to serve on juries. In the November 1920 election, 26 million American women voted for the first time.

Women again took men's jobs during World War II. But when the war ended in 1945, the women did not want to leave these jobs. They wanted good jobs, equal pay for equal work, and the right to work in any occupation.

Sandra Day O'Connor was one woman who wanted a "man's" job. She wanted to be a lawyer. In 1949 she went to law school. There were only three women in her class of 100 students. She was one of the best

Sandra Day O'Connor

students, but when she graduated she had trouble finding a job. Law firms wanted to hire her as a secretary, not a lawyer. She finally found a job as a county lawyer in California and later as a lawyer for the state of Arizona. In 1981 she became the first woman justice of the United States Supreme Court.

Today in the U.S., women are doctors, scientists, lawyers, and presidents of companies. Women serve in the Senate and the House of Representatives. They also have had some of the most important jobs in government, such as Attorney General and Secretary of State. In the 21st century, a woman's place is any place she wants to be.

▶ What did you read?

Circle the main idea.

a. Women can vote and have many different jobs in the U.S.

b. Women's rights have changed over the years in the U.S.

▶ Read again

Are these sentences true? Find the answers in the reading. Circle *yes* or *no*. If the answer is not in the reading, circle *doesn't say*. Check your answers with a partner.

1. In 1776 women had the same rights as men.	yes	(no)	doesn't say
2. In 1776 women could own houses.	yes	no	doesn't say
3. In the 1830s women wanted the right to vote.	yes	no	doesn't say
4. Before the Civil War most women worked at home.	yes	no	doesn't say
5. After the Civil War all of the states let women own houses.	yes	no	doesn't say
6. After World War I, women got the right to vote.	yes	no	doesn't say
7. After World War II, women got equal pay for equal work.	yes	no	doesn't say
8. It was easy for Sandra Day O'Connor to find a job.	yes	no	doesn't say

▶ Show you understand

Match the dates on the time line with the sentences. Find the information in the reading. Then use the time line to tell the history of women's rights to your partner. Add other details you remember.

Time Line of Women's Rights in the United States

a. The Civil War began. Women took men's jobs.

b. The U.S. became a country. Women didn't have equal rights.

c. Women can have any job.

1776
1830
1861
1920
1945
Today

d. Women's groups began to fight for rights.

e. World War II ended. Women wanted equal pay for equal work.

f. Women voted for the first time.

▶ Talk more about it

Think about these questions. Then discuss your ideas.

> 1. Some people think "A woman's place is in the home." Do you agree? Why or why not?
>
> 2. Should there be "men's" jobs and "women's" jobs? Why or why not?
>
> 3. Should women work in government? Why or why not? Do women work in government in your country? If so, talk about them.

After You Read

▶ Outline

Complete this outline. Fill in the blanks with the correct main ideas from the box.

> Things began to change.
>
> Today women have equal rights.
>
> In 1776 women did not have many rights.

A Woman's Place

I. _____

    A. A husband owned his wife.

    B. Women could not vote.

    C. Women could not own houses.

II. _____

    A. War made many women take "men's" jobs.

    B. Women fought for their rights.

    C. Women wanted good jobs and equal pay.

III. _____

    A. Women have the right to vote.

    B. Women have the right to own houses.

    C. Women have the right to serve on juries.

▶ *Puzzle*

**Read the sentences below. Find the words in the box that go in each blank.
Write the words in the puzzle. Follow the example.**

owned	fight	rights	pay	century	~~vote~~	managers

1. v o t e

2. _ _ _ _ _ _

3. _ _ _ _ _ _ _

4. _ _ _ _ _

5. _ _ _ _ _

6. _ _ _ _ _ _ _ _

7. _ _ _

What is the secret word? _____

1. After World War I, women got the right to _____ .

2. In 1776 women couldn't own a house. They couldn't vote. They didn't have _____ .

3. In the 21st _____ , a woman's place is any place she wants it to be.

4. Women had to _____ for their rights.

5. In 1776 a man _____ his house, his wife, and his children.

6. Some women were _____ of farms and businesses.

7. Women wanted equal _____ for equal work.

Before You Read

Look at the pictures and the captions on pages 73 and 74. Look at the title of the reading. Answer the questions.

1. How many people is this reading about? _____

2. Why are these people important? _____

While You Read

Choose two women to read about. Check your answers while you read.

Dr. Gertrude Belle Elion
Biochemist
1918–

Dr. Gertrude Belle Elion studied biology and chemistry at New York University. She graduated in 1941 but had trouble finding a job. When World War II started, many men joined the Army and it was easier for women scientists to get work. Dr. Elion got a job as a chemist and developed medications to treat cancer, malaria, and other diseases. Her work also helped other scientists find ways to treat AIDS. She won the Nobel Prize in medicine in 1988, when she was 70 years old.

Dr. Mae C. Jemison
Astronaut
1956–

Dr. Mae C. Jemison has many interests. She studied both chemical engineering and African-American studies at Stanford University and received two bachelor's degrees. She also studied dance and theater arts. Then she went to Cornell Medical School and became a doctor. She practiced medicine for six years. In 1986 she applied to NASA's astronaut program along with 2,000 other people. She was one of 15 people chosen, and she became the first female African-American astronaut. In 1992 she rode a shuttle into space for an eight-day flight. Since then she has been a professor at Dartmouth College.

Maria Goeppert Mayer
Physicist
1906–1972

Dr. Maria Goeppert Mayer was born in Kattowitz, Germany. She studied mathematics and physics at the University of Gottingen. In 1930 she received a doctorate in physics. She moved to the United States and tried to get a job as a professor. They didn't want to hire a woman, so she studied on her own and made some important discoveries about the structure of atoms. She also wrote a textbook. In 1959 she finally got a job at a university. Four years later she won the Nobel Prize in physics for her work with atoms.

Maria Mitchell
Astronomer
1818–1889

Maria Mitchell was a librarian during the day, but at night she took out her telescope and studied the planets and stars. One night in 1847 she saw a bright star that looked like it had a tail. It was a new comet. This discovery made her a famous astronomer. Soon she became the first professor of astronomy at Vassar College. Professor Mitchell was also the director of the college's observatory. There she and her students studied the sun, Saturn, and Jupiter. She was the first woman elected to the Academy of Arts and Sciences.

Antonia Novello
Surgeon General
1944–

Dr. Antonia Novello studied medicine in San Juan, Puerto Rico, and became a pediatrician. She saw many children who did not get the health care they needed. Because she wanted everyone to get good health care, she went to work for the U.S.

National Institutes of Health (NIH). Dr. Novello studied how AIDS hurt women and their babies. She also warned children not to smoke or drink alcohol. In 1990 she became the first woman and the first Hispanic to become the Surgeon General of the United States.

Ellen Swallow Richards
Chemist
1842– 1911

Ellen Swallow Richards was the first woman to study at the Massachusetts Institute of Technology (MIT). Her friends said she knew as much as an encyclopedia, so they called her Ellencyclopedia. She was very interested in the environment. She studied water and air pollution and called the study of the environment ecology. In 1882 she published a book called *The Chemistry of Cooking and Cleaning*. Dr. Richards believed science could make homes safer and cleaner, so she developed a new area of study called home economics. In home economics classes she taught women about health and hygiene in the home.

Dr. Chien-Shiung Wu
Physicist
1912– 1997

Dr. Chien-Shiung Wu left Shanghai, China, to study for her doctorate in nuclear physics at the University of California at Berkeley. She wanted to be like the French physicist, Madame Marie Curie. During World War II, Dr. Wu helped develop the first atomic bomb. In 1956 she did an experiment that changed the way scientists thought about physics. Her revolutionary work made her famous. In 1957 she became a professor of physics at Columbia University and encouraged young women to study science.

▶ What did you read?

The words below make a sentence about the main idea of the reading. Put them in the correct order and write the sentence on the line.

scientists   women   are   ~~There~~   great   many

There _____ .

▶ Read again

Fill in the chart for the scientists you read about. Use the reading to help you.

Scientist	Her job	Two important things she did
1. Dr. Gertrude Belle Elion	Biochemist	She developed medications for cancer. She also…
2. Dr. Mae C. Jemison		
3. Dr. Maria Goeppert Mayer		
4. Maria Mitchell		
5. Dr. Antonia Novello		
6. Dr. Ellen Swallow Richards		
7. Dr. Chien-Shiung Wu		

▶ Show you understand

Walk around the class. Find people who read about the scientists you did not read about. Ask them the questions and complete the chart on page 75. Then check your answers with a partner.

▶ Read more

Now read about the rest of the scientists on pages 73 and 74.

▶ Talk more about it

Think about these questions. Then discuss your ideas.

1. Why was it difficult in the past for many women scientists to get work?

2. Who is a famous woman scientist you know about? What did she study? What made her famous?

After You Read
▶ Write

Make a mind map for one of the scientists from the reading. First write her name in the center circle. Next write her occupation and areas of study on the correct lines. Then write three or four facts about her on the other lines. Use the reading to help you.

_____

occupation

_____

_____

_____

name

_____

area of study

_____

 Turn to _Remember the Words_ at the back of this book.

TALK ABOUT IT

A. **Work in a small group. Look at the categories in the chart. Brainstorm a list of plants you know and fill in the chart. Then add two of your own categories and complete the chart. Some plants can go in more than one category.**

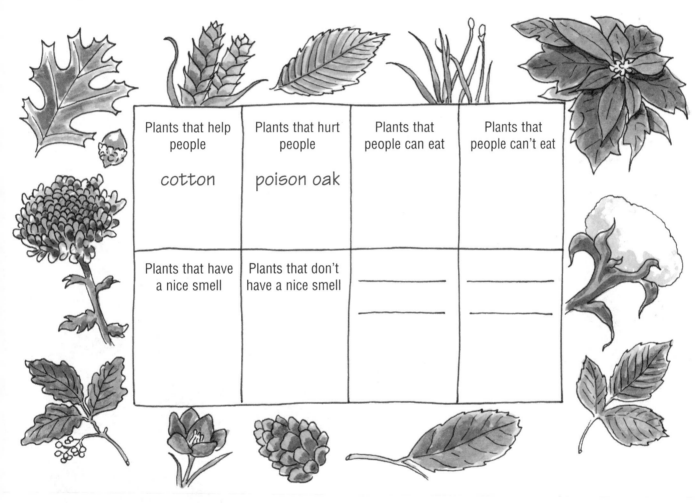

Plants that help people	Plants that hurt people	Plants that people can eat	Plants that people can't eat
cotton	poison oak		
Plants that have a nice smell	Plants that don't have a nice smell	_____ _____	_____ _____

B. **Think about these questions. Then ask and answer the questions with a partner.**

1. What is your favorite plant or flower? Why?

2. What is the most unusual plant or flower you know? Why is it unusual? What does it look like?

3. How do some plants hurt people?

Before You Read

Look at the pictures and the captions. Look at the title of the reading. Guess the answers to the questions.

1. What happened between January 1998 and July 1998?

_____

2. In which area of the United States did it happen? Why do you think so?

_____

While You Read

Read this magazine article. Think about your guesses while you read.

Kudzu

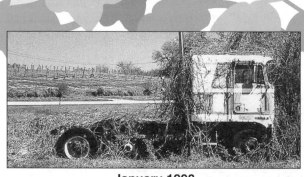
January 1998

July 1998

One warm day in January, Tim Sanders' truck broke down on the highway near Greenville, Alabama. He got a ride home, but he didn't have enough money to tow the truck into town. He and a friend went back to get the truck, but they couldn't find it. Several months later they tried again. They drove up and down. Then they stopped near a large hill of vines by the side of the road. Tim took out an ax and started to cut away the vines. There was his truck. In just six months kudzu vines had covered it completely!

Kudzu is a plant native to Japan and China. It is a vine with large, green leaves and small, purple flowers. The roots of one plant sometimes weigh 200 pounds (441 kg) and lie 10–12 feet (3–3.6 m) deep in the ground.

In 1876 the Japanese government brought kudzu to the United States as part of a plant show. American gardeners thought it was beautiful and began to plant it everywhere. Some gardeners found that animals liked to eat it and told farmers to plant it to feed goats, cows, and horses. In the 1930s the U.S. government paid people to plant kudzu to protect the soil. The government scientists didn't know that kudzu grows very quickly in the warm weather of the Southeastern United States.

In the summer kudzu can grow one foot

kudzu

a day or up to 60 feet in a season. It now covers 7 million acres of land in the South. It covers anything that is not moving: homes, cars, and telephone poles. It takes over whole fields so that nothing else can grow. Some forests are dying because kudzu blocks out the light that the trees need to live. No birds or animals can live in a forest covered with kudzu.

Now the government is trying to kill the kudzu. Scientists tried poisons, but the kudzu did not die. It just grew faster. Scientists have found one kind of caterpillar in the South that eats kudzu. They are also thinking about bringing some insects from China. These insects like to eat kudzu, but they might eat other plants, too. This might cause new problems.

For now, kudzu is here to stay. So if you visit the South, don't leave your car by the side of the road. If you do, you might need an ax to find it! ■

▶ *What did you read?*

Choose another title for this reading. Circle the best one.

a. Plant Covers the South

b. Ways to Kill Kudzu

▶ *Read again*

Read these questions. Find the answers in the reading. Write them in the blanks. Then check your answers with a partner.

1. How long did it take the kudzu to cover Tim Sanders' truck? _____six months_____

2. How did Tim find his truck? _____

3. Where does kudzu come from? _____

4. How much can the roots weigh? _____

5. When did kudzu first come to the U.S.? _____

6. What might scientists use to kill kudzu? _____

▶ *Show you understand*

Complete each sentence. Write the letters of your answers in the blanks.

__d__ 1. Tim got a ride home

_____ 2. Tim couldn't find his truck

_____ 3. People planted kudzu

_____ 4. Kudzu grows well in the South

_____ 5. Forests are dying

_____ 6. Scientists might bring insects from China

a. because the weather is wet and warm.

b. because kudzu blocks out the light.

c. because it was covered with kudzu.

d. because his truck broke down.

e. because they want to kill the kudzu.

f. because they wanted to feed animals and protect the soil.

▶ *Talk more about it*

Think about these questions. Then discuss your ideas.

1. Why is the U.S. government trying to kill kudzu? Give three reasons.

2. Plants that are not native to a country often cause problems. Should governments kill those plants? Why or why not? Use kudzu as one example.

3. What are some plants in your country that cause problems? What problems do they cause? Are people trying to kill those plants? Why or why not?

After You Read

▶ *Words, words, words*

Read the sentences. What do the underlined words mean? Look for clues in the reading. Write the letters of the correct meanings in the blanks.

    a. measurement of land equal to 4,840 square yards   **d.** all over

    b. that naturally grows in   ~~**e.**~~ stopped working

    c. chemicals that can hurt or kill plants   **f.** doesn't let light go through

  e   **1.** Tim Sanders' truck <u>broke down</u> on the highway.

_____ **2.** In just six months kudzu vines had covered it <u>completely</u>.

_____ **3.** Kudzu is a plant <u>native to</u> Japan and China.

_____ **4.** It now covers 7 million <u>acres</u> of land in the South.

_____ **5.** Some forests are dying because kudzu <u>blocks out</u> the light...

_____ **6.** Scientists tried <u>poisons</u>, but the kudzu did not die.

▶ *Write an outline*

Copy this outline on your own paper. Fill in the blanks with the correct details from the box.

kills forests	feeds animals	grows 1 foot a day	scientists tried poisons
	native to Japan, China		

——— Kudzu ———

I. Characteristics
   A. <u>native to Japan, China</u>
   B. green leaves, purple flowers
   C. _____

III. Problems
   A. covers everything
   B. nothing else can grow
   C. _____

II. Uses
   A. decoration
   B. _____
   C. protects soil

IV. Solutions
   A. _____
   B. one caterpillar eats kudzu
   C. bring insects from China

Before You Read

Look at the pictures. Look at the readings and the titles on pages 83 and 85. Guess the answers to these questions.

1. What kind of readings are these?

    a. pages from a history book   **b.** folktales   **c.** poems

2. What is the king doing?

    _____

3. Who is the man behind the tree? How does he feel? Why?

    _____

Jigsaw Reading

Form teams of four students. Number off 1–4. Students 1 and 2 become partners and read "The Real Flower" on page 83. Students 3 and 4 become partners and read "The Witch and the Rosebushes" on page 85.

Read this selection. Think about your guesses while you read.

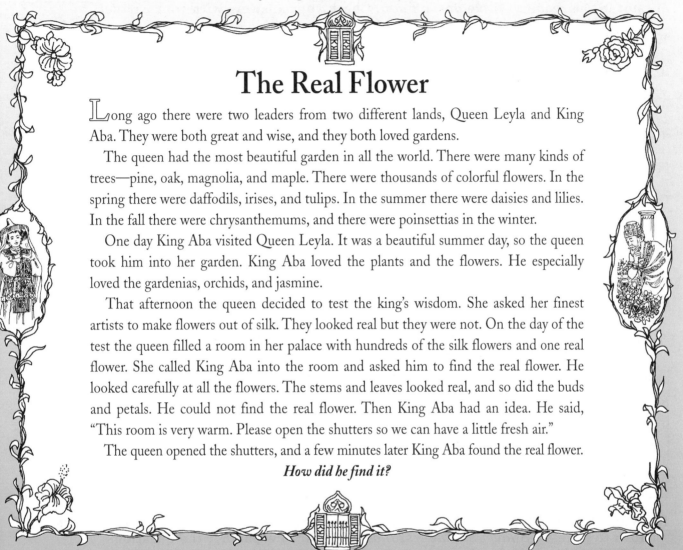

The Real Flower

Long ago there were two leaders from two different lands, Queen Leyla and King Aba. They were both great and wise, and they both loved gardens.

The queen had the most beautiful garden in all the world. There were many kinds of trees—pine, oak, magnolia, and maple. There were thousands of colorful flowers. In the spring there were daffodils, irises, and tulips. In the summer there were daisies and lilies. In the fall there were chrysanthemums, and there were poinsettias in the winter.

One day King Aba visited Queen Leyla. It was a beautiful summer day, so the queen took him into her garden. King Aba loved the plants and the flowers. He especially loved the gardenias, orchids, and jasmine.

That afternoon the queen decided to test the king's wisdom. She asked her finest artists to make flowers out of silk. They looked real but they were not. On the day of the test the queen filled a room in her palace with hundreds of the silk flowers and one real flower. She called King Aba into the room and asked him to find the real flower. He looked carefully at all the flowers. The stems and leaves looked real, and so did the buds and petals. He could not find the real flower. Then King Aba had an idea. He said, "This room is very warm. Please open the shutters so we can have a little fresh air."

The queen opened the shutters, and a few minutes later King Aba found the real flower.

How did he find it?

Work with your partner to guess the answer. Then check your answer on page 114.

▶ *What did you read?*

Circle the main idea.

a. A wise person can find the truth.   **b.** Queen Leyla and King Aba loved gardens.

Now do the exercises on page 84.

► Read again

Are these sentences true? Find answers in the reading. Circle *yes* or *no*. If the answers are not in the reading, circle *doesn't say*. Check your answers with your partner.

1.	The queen and king were both wise.	(yes)	no	doesn't say
2.	They were husband and wife.	yes	no	doesn't say
3.	The king had a beautiful garden.	yes	no	doesn't say
4.	The queen's garden had flowers all year long.	yes	no	doesn't say
5.	The king wanted to test the queen.	yes	no	doesn't say
6.	The queen's artists made real flowers.	yes	no	doesn't say
7.	The test was to find the real flower.	yes	no	doesn't say
8.	The king found the real flower.	yes	no	doesn't say

► Show you understand

A. Work with your partner to answer the questions for the story you both read. Write the answers in the chart.

The Real Flower	
1. Who are the people in the folktale?	Queen Leyla...
2. Where does the folktale take place?	
3. What is the man's problem?	

B. Change partners. Now students 1 and 3 are partners. Students 2 and 4 are partners. Turn to page 86, *Show you understand*. Ask your new partner the questions and fill in the chart for the story he or she read.

► Read more

Now students 1 and 2 read "The Witch and the Rosebushes" on page 85.
Students 3 and 4 read "The Real Flower" on page 83.

Read this selection. Think about your guesses while you read.

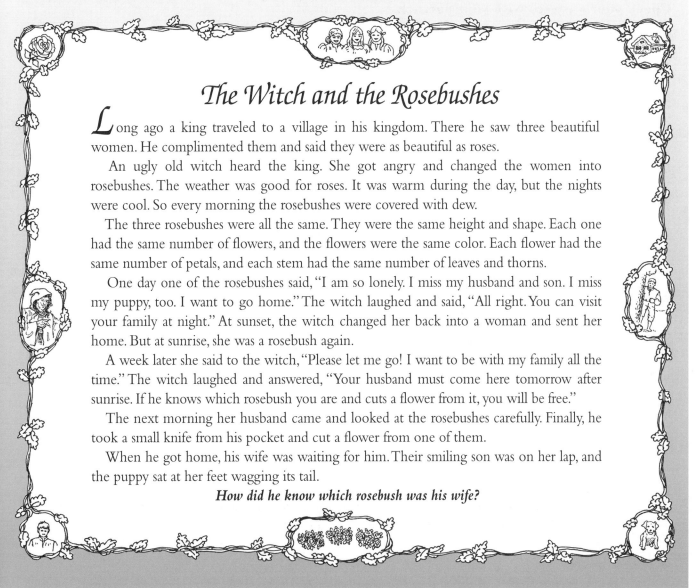

The Witch and the Rosebushes

Long ago a king traveled to a village in his kingdom. There he saw three beautiful women. He complimented them and said they were as beautiful as roses.

An ugly old witch heard the king. She got angry and changed the women into rosebushes. The weather was good for roses. It was warm during the day, but the nights were cool. So every morning the rosebushes were covered with dew.

The three rosebushes were all the same. They were the same height and shape. Each one had the same number of flowers, and the flowers were the same color. Each flower had the same number of petals, and each stem had the same number of leaves and thorns.

One day one of the rosebushes said, "I am so lonely. I miss my husband and son. I miss my puppy, too. I want to go home." The witch laughed and said, "All right. You can visit your family at night." At sunset, the witch changed her back into a woman and sent her home. But at sunrise, she was a rosebush again.

A week later she said to the witch, "Please let me go! I want to be with my family all the time." The witch laughed and answered, "Your husband must come here tomorrow after sunrise. If he knows which rosebush you are and cuts a flower from it, you will be free."

The next morning her husband came and looked at the rosebushes carefully. Finally, he took a small knife from his pocket and cut a flower from one of them.

When he got home, his wife was waiting for him. Their smiling son was on her lap, and the puppy sat at her feet wagging its tail.

How did he know which rosebush was his wife?

Work with your partner to guess the answer. Then check your answer on page 114.

▶ *What did you read?*

Circle the main idea.

a. A witch gets angry.   **b.** A smart husband solves a problem.

> Now do the exercises on page 86.

▶ *Read again*

Complete these sentences. Find the answers in the reading. Circle *a* or *b*.
Check your answers with your partner.

1. The women lived in a   **(a.)** small village.   **b.** small city.

2. They were as beautiful as   **a.** bushes.   **b.** roses.

3. The witch was   **a.** kind.   **b.** not kind.

4. The three rosebushes looked   **a.** different.   **b.** alike.

5. One woman wanted to visit   **a.** her family.   **b.** her village.

6. She wanted to be with them   **a.** all night.   **b.** all the time.

7. At the end of the story the husband felt   **a.** relieved.   **b.** worried.

▶ *Show you understand*

A. Work with your partner to answer the questions for the story you both read.
Write the answers in the chart.

The Witch and the Rosebushes	
1. Who are the people in the folktale?	the witch...
2. Where does the folktale take place?	
3. What is the man's problem?	

B. Change partners. Now students 1 and 3 are partners. Students 2 and 4 are partners.
Turn to page 84, *Show you understand*. Ask your new partner the questions and fill in
the chart for the story he or she read.

▶ *Read more*

> Now students 1 and 2 read "The Witch and the Rosebushes" on page 85.
> Students 3 and 4 read "The Real Flower" on page 83.

 Turn to *Remember the Words* at the back of this book.

TALK ABOUT IT

A. Work with a group. Look at the graph and the chart. Read the graph to find at least one job that fits each category in the chart. Write them.

Here are 15 occupations with many job opportunities and high pay.

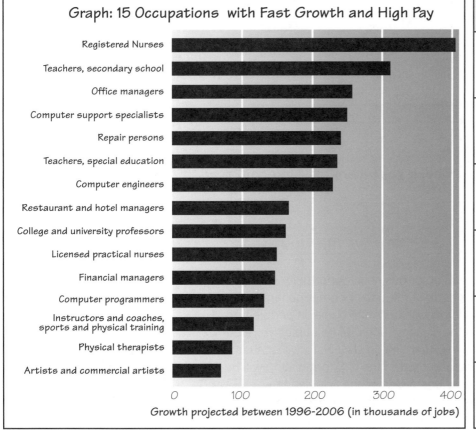

Graph: 15 Occupations with Fast Growth and High Pay

- Registered Nurses
- Teachers, secondary school
- Office managers
- Computer support specialists
- Repair persons
- Teachers, special education
- Computer engineers
- Restaurant and hotel managers
- College and university professors
- Licensed practical nurses
- Financial managers
- Computer programmers
- Instructors and coaches, sports and physical training
- Physical therapists
- Artists and commercial artists

0   100   200   300   400

Growth projected between 1996-2006 (in thousands of jobs)

Chart

Computer Technology

Education

Finance

Travel and Hospitality

Nutrition and Fitness

Health Care

B. Think about these questions. Then ask and answer the questions with a partner.

1. Imagine your friend is deciding on an occupation. What information from the graph would you give him or her? Give at least three facts.

2. Would you like one of the jobs in the graph? Why or why not? If yes, what kind of education, training, or work experience would you need to get the job?

READ ABOUT IT

While You Read

Read this Web page. Check your answers while you read.

Work for the Future

Are you looking for a great job or business opportunity? Choose an occupation that meets the needs of the baby boomer generation!

The baby boomer generation includes the 76 million people born between 1946 and 1964 in the United States. More babies were born during those years than in any other time in U.S. history. Because there are so many baby boomers, one-third of the U.S. population will be 50 or older by 2010. In 1991 only one-fourth of the population was over 50.

Companies across the nation are preparing for this big change. There will be many job and business opportunities for people who can meet the needs of older baby boomers. Here is a list of the five best job categories. Use it to get ideas for jobs or for starting your own business.

1. Finance—Many baby boomers make a good living. They began working at a time when there were many good jobs. They need help saving their money for retirement. They need accountants and financial planners to help them plan for the future.

2. Sales—Many baby boomers have better salaries now than when they were younger. They have more money to spend, so they can buy many things. By 2004 sales of clothing, furniture, and electronics will go up 30%. Jobs in sales will go up 20%. There will be many opportunities to start new businesses, especially in mail-order or Internet sales. These businesses will need sales representatives, telemarketers, salespeople, and Webmasters to sell their products.

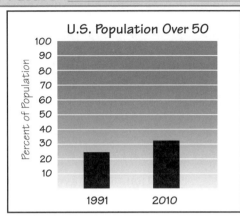

U.S. Population Over 50

(bar graph: y-axis labeled "Percent of Population" from 10 to 100; x-axis shows 1991 at about 25% and 2010 at about 33%)

3. Travel and Hospitality—Baby boomers will travel more after they retire. The travel business will need pilots and flight attendants. Hotels will need to hire more managers, desk clerks, housekeepers, and bellhops. If you can serve customers, you will find a good job. It may also be a good time to open your own restaurant.

4. Nutrition and Fitness—Baby boomers care about their health and how they look. There is a need for new health clubs and weight-loss clinics. These new health clubs need managers and aerobics instructors. Weight-loss clinics will employ more dieticians and counselors to help people learn about nutrition. Baby boomers may be getting older, but they want to look and feel great!

5. Health Care—As these large numbers of baby boomers get older, they will need medical care. There will be many jobs for health-care managers and nurses. Elderly people will need home attendants to assist them. There will be a need for nursing homes, medical clinics, doctors, and dentists. By 2005, 10% of all U.S. workers will work in health-care services. And 17% of all new jobs will be health-care jobs. That means 3.1 million new jobs!

Now is the time to find a great occupation or start your own business. Don't let these opportunities pass you by. Good luck in your search!

▶ *What did you read?*

Circle the main idea.

a. Large numbers of older adults will make jobs grow in five areas.

b. Older adults will be working in five job areas.

▶ *Read again*

**Are these sentences true? Find the answers in the reading. Circle *yes* or *no*.
Check your answers with a partner.**

1. There are 76 million baby boomers in the U.S.   (yes)   no

2. By 2010, about 30% of the population will be over 50.   yes   no

3. Accountants help people save for retirement.   yes   no

4. Jobs in sales will go up by 30%.   yes   no

5. The travel business is growing.   yes   no

6. By 2005, 10% of all new jobs will be in health care.   yes   no

7. People in these occupations will have many job or business opportunities.   yes   no

▶ *Show you understand*

Complete each sentence. Write the letters of your answers in the blanks.

_C_ **1.** The baby boomer generation has that name

_____ **2.** There will be many business opportunities

_____ **3.** Many baby boomers make a good living

_____ **4.** Hotels will need more employees

_____ **5.** There will be more jobs in health care

_____ **6.** Health clubs need more aerobics instructors

a. because baby boomers want to exercise.

b. because they began working when there were many good jobs.

c. because between 1946 and 1964 more people were born in the U.S. than ever before.

d. because of a big change in the number of older adults.

e. because baby boomers will travel more when they retire.

f. because the large numbers of baby boomers will need medical care.

▶ *Talk more about it*

Think about these questions. Then discuss your ideas.

1. How do changes in the population make new jobs? What other changes make new jobs?

2. Would you like to have one of the jobs or businesses in this reading? Why or why not?

After You Read

▶ *Words, words, words*

A. Read the sentences. What do the underlined words mean? Look for clues in the reading. Write the letters of the correct meanings in the blanks.

    a. getting ready   **d.** the time after people stop working

    b. chances   **e.** get a good salary

    c. eating healthy food   ~~**f.**~~ people living in a place

_f_ **1.** In 1991 only one-quarter of the <u>population</u> was over 50.

____ **2.** Companies across the nation are <u>preparing</u> for this big change.

____ **3.** There will be many job and business <u>opportunities</u> for people who can meet the needs of older baby boomers.

____ **4.** Many baby boomers <u>make a good living</u>.

____ **5.** They need help saving their money for <u>retirement</u>.

____ **6.** Weight-loss clinics will employ more dietitians and counselors to help people learn about <u>nutrition</u>.

B. Study this word family. Look at the examples. Then fill in the blanks with the correct words.

Word Family	Examples
retire *verb*	Baby boomers will travel more after they *retire*.
retirement *noun*	They need help saving their money for *retirement*.

      My mom is going to _____ soon. She's planning to relax, play golf, and travel during her _____. She's really looking forward to it.

 The travel industry is growing by 40% a year. By 2007 there will be 100 million more jobs in the travel industry. Travel and tourism is the third largest industry in the U.S.

Before You Read

Look at the pictures and the captions. Look at the title and the headings of the reading. Guess the answers to the questions.

1. What is this reading about?

   _____

2. How do these people make a living?

   _____

While You Read

Read this magazine article. Think about your guesses while you read.

Make It Your Business

The job world is changing. In 1995, two-thirds of workers in the United States had jobs with regular hours, medical benefits, and retirement plans. Only one-third of them owned their own businesses in that year. By the year 2010, one-half of all workers in the United States will have their own businesses. If you are looking for a new job or occupation, think about starting your own business.

How can you open your own business? Learn from these experienced business people.

CD SUCCESS

Brian Tran was a 15-year-old student, but he didn't like school. He wanted to make money. He began to look for an after-school job. Most of his

Brian does everything he can to make his customers happy.

friends had jobs as delivery people or salesclerks, but Brian didn't want to do those jobs. He wanted to do something he liked, so he decided to start his own business.

Brian liked music, so he borrowed a CD player and some speakers. He started working as a DJ at his friends' parties for $25 a night. He wanted to buy his own electronic equipment, but he wasn't making enough money. Then he found out about a university program that helps young business owners. There he met a professor who gave him some good advice. She told him that he should stop working at his friends' parties. She said Brian could make $400 or $500 a night playing music for weddings or school dances. Brian learned some simple business rules from the professor, too. She told him he should always be on time and do everything he could to make his customers happy.

Today Brian makes about $2,000 a month. He plans to use his money for college after he graduates from high school. Now he has a reason to go to college. He wants to study accounting, marketing, and advertising. He loves his business and wants to learn how to make it grow.

TRASH INTO CASH

Mara Fleischer and her husband, Sean Penrith, were cleaning up their house after a party. They were throwing away several beverage bottles when Mara said, "It makes me sad to throw these bottles away. The colors and shapes are so beautiful." Mara, a designer, began to think of ways to use the bottles. Soon she had an idea. She cut off the bottom of a bottle and turned the bottle upside down. Then she glued the two pieces together. When she was finished, she had a beautiful and unusual wine glass.

Sean, an engineer, thought it would be easy to manufacture these new glasses, but he was wrong. He couldn't find a good way to keep the two pieces together. He and Mara worked on the problem in their small garage near Johannesburg, South Africa. Mara's brother, Philip Tetley, helped them. After eight months, they invented a new way to put the glass pieces together. Then they each put in $100 and started to manufacture the glasses.

Now they make glasses, vases, candlesticks, and lamps from recycled glass. Their Green Glass products are becoming popular around the world because they are useful, beautiful, and they help the environment.

The people in these stories made great businesses from simple ideas. Do you have a good idea? Maybe you, too, can start a business of your own.

Mara, Sean, and Phillip started their successful Green Glass business with $100 each.

TIPS FOR STARTING YOUR OWN BUSINESS

- Choose a business or service people need.
- Choose a business you love.
- Be different. Do something so customers will notice your business.
- Do everything you can to make customers happy.

▶ *What did you read?*

The words below make a sentence about the main idea of the reading. Put them in the correct order and write the sentence on the line.

| ~~Simple~~ | make | can | often | successful | businesses | ideas |

Simple _____ .

▶ *Read again*

Complete these sentences. Find the answers in the reading. Circle *a* or *b*.

1. In 1995, two-thirds of workers in the U.S. had   **a.** businesses.   **(b.)** jobs.

2. By 2010, one-half of all U.S. workers will have   **a.** benefits.   **b.** businesses.

3. Brian is a DJ because he likes   **a.** parties.   **b.** music.

4. A professor gave Brian   **a.** advice.   **b.** equipment.

5. The name of the company is Green Glass because the bottles are   **a.** green.   **b.** recycled.

6. Manufacturing the glasses was   **a.** easy.   **b.** difficult.

7. The Green Glass company began with   **a.** $100.   **b.** $300.

▶ *Talk more about it*

Think about these questions. Then discuss your ideas.

> 1. What can Brian do to make his customers notice his business?
>
> 2. How is the Green Glass company different from other glass companies?
>
> 3. Would you like to start your own business? Why or why not?

▶ *Write*

Answer question 1 on your own paper. List as many things as you can. Then work with a partner to answer questions 2 and 3.

1. What do you do for recreation?	2. What are some skills you use or things you make?	3. How could you make money using these skills or things?
play soccer	kick and pass the ball, know the rules	coach kids be a referee
knit	knit baby blankets, scarves, and hats	sell them at flea markets give knitting lessons

 Turn to *Remember the Words* at the back of this book.

TALK ABOUT IT

A. Work with a partner. Look at the picture. Discuss the questions and write the answers.

1. What is the woman doing?

_____

2. What is she dreaming about?

_____

3. Do you think her dreams will come true? Why or why not?

_____

B. Think about these questions. Then ask and answer the questions with your partner.

1. What do you dream about doing?

2. Why do you want to do it?

3. How can you make your dream come true?

Before You Read

Look at the pictures. Look at the titles and the headings of the readings on pages 97 and 98. Guess the answers to the questions.

1. What kind of readings are these?

_____

2. Why is the title *Dream Adventures*?

_____

Jigsaw Reading

Form teams of four students. Number off 1–4. Students 1 and 2 become partners and read about *Dream Adventures*, Scuba Diving on page 97. Students 3 and 4 become partners and read about *Dream Adventures*, Backpacking on page 98.

While You Read

Read this selection. Think about your guesses while you read.

Bicycle Trips
Canoeing Camps
Fishing Camps*
Hiking & Backpacking Trips
Race-Car Driving Courses
Sailboarding Schools
Scuba Diving Courses
Ski Schools*
Skydiving Schools*
Tennis Camps

*Physically challenged people
 can attend

Dream Adventures

What is your dream adventure? Do you want to hike the Grand Canyon? Do you want to jump out of a plane or learn to drive a race car? Do you want to go scuba diving in Costa Rica? You can! From biking to canoeing, from skiing to sailboarding, *Dream Adventures* has it all!

Find a camp, course, or trip that is just right for you and make your dream come true!

Learn Scuba Diving with Blue Sail Sports in Costa Rica

Do you dream of swimming with fish in warm ocean waters or exploring underwater caves? Do you want to see Costa Rica's famous manta rays and white-tip sharks? Then a Blue Sail Sports Scuba Diving Adventure is for you! If you can swim, you can learn to scuba dive in only four days! Become one of the 5 million certified scuba divers in the world. Your four-day course can start any day of the week. There is one instructor for every four students. The complete four-day course costs $395 per person. This fabulous price includes diving mask, snorkel, fins, wet suit, and scuba tank. **Call 800/555-1212 or fax 808/555-4916 today!**

Now do the exercises on page 99.

While You Read

Read this selection. Think about your guesses while you read.

Bicycle Trips
Canoeing Camps
Fishing Camps*
Hiking & Backpacking Trips
Race-Car Driving Courses
Sailboarding Schools
Scuba Diving Courses
Ski Schools*
Skydiving Schools*
Tennis Camps

*Physically challenged people
 can attend

Dream Adventures

What is your dream adventure? Do you want to hike the Grand Canyon? Do you want to jump out of a plane or learn to drive a race car? Do you want to go backpacking in the beautiful Canadian Rocky Mountains? You can! From biking to canoeing, from skiing to sailboarding, *Dream Adventures* has it all!

Find a camp, course, or trip that is just right for you and make your dream come true!

Go Backpacking in the Canadian Rockies

Visit Canada's beautiful Rocky Mountains. Go hiking in green forests and fishing in clear blue lakes. Watch for wild animals like moose and bighorn sheep. See big birds like the bald eagle. Each day you'll hike 8–10 miles (12–16 km). One day you'll see high waterfalls and rushing rivers. Another day you'll climb mountain peaks.

Experienced guides lead each group of 15 hikers and teach you about backpacking. They give you information on plants and animals in the area. In July and August we have 7-day trips starting at $475. This fabulous price includes tents, camping stoves, and lanterns. Hikers need to bring their own sleeping bags, foam pads, and backpacks. Trips for beginning to advanced hikers. Call or fax Canadian Climbers Club,
TEL 888/555-1212   FAX 415/555-7579.

Now do the exercises on page 99.

▶ What did you read?

The words below make a sentence about the main idea of the reading. Put them in the correct order and write the sentence on the line.

| do | things | ~~People~~ | recreation | for | can | exciting | many |

___People_____ .

▶ Read again

Are these sentences true? Find the answers in the reading. Circle *yes* or *no*. Check your answers with your partner.

1. People can make their dreams come true with *Dream Adventures*.   (yes)   no

2. Anyone can learn to sky dive.   yes   no

3. *Dream Adventures* has a surfing camp.   yes   no

4. There are eight different camps, classes, or trips in the ad.   yes   no

5. People can go on *Dream Adventures* in many places in the world.   yes   no

6. People on *Dream Adventures* sometimes see animals.   yes   no

▶ Show you understand

A. Work with your partner to answer the questions about the Web page advertisement you read. Write the answers in the correct column.

	Scuba Diving	Backpacking
1. Where is the course or trip?	Costa Rica	Canadian Rockies
2. How long is the course/trip?		
3. What animals might people see?		
4. What else will people see?		
5. How many people will be in each group?		
6. How much does it cost?		
7. What does the price include?		

B. Now change partners. Students 1 and 3 are partners and students 2 and 4 are partners. Ask your new partner the questions and fill in the chart for the ad he or she read.

► *Read more*

Now students 1 and 2 read about *Dream Adventures*, Backpacking on page 98. Students 3 and 4 read about *Dream Adventures*, Scuba Diving on page 97.

► *Talk more about it*

Think about these questions. Then discuss your ideas.

1. Do you think recreation is important? Why or why not?
2. Which camps, courses, or trips on this Web page would you like to try? Why?

After You Read

► *Puzzle*

Read the sentences below. Find the words in the box that go in each blank. Write the words in the puzzle. Follow the example.

adventure   exploring   famous   certified   clear   guide   rushing

Down

1. Her ___ was an unusual and exciting experience.
2. The person who leads the trip is the ___.
3. The lake is so ___ you can see the bottom.
4. He was ___ the cave to find out what was there.

Across

5. He finished the training course and became a ___ guide.
6. The ___ water moved very quickly.
7. Everyone knows about the ___ manta rays.

Before You Read

Look at the pictures on pages 101 and 102. Look at the title of the reading. Guess the answer to the question.

Why is the title of this reading "I Can!"?

_____

While You Read

Read this magazine article. Think about your guess while you read.

I Can!

Kacey McCallister

Kacey McCallister always dreamed of playing basketball on the Boys' Club team. At first the coach wouldn't let him play play, so Kacey practiced hard. Now he is on the team, but he is not the best player. This 11-year-old boy can dribble and pass as well as the other kids, but he moves up and down the court more slowly. And shooting a basket is difficult for Kacey because he has no legs.

Kacey lost both legs in an accident. When he was six, he ran into the street and a tractor trailer hit him. But Kacey doesn't let his physical challenge stop him from doing the things he loves. He has learned to play many sports. In basketball he dribbles the ball with one hand and uses his other hand to move his body around the court. Kacey also plays baseball. He can catch and throw the ball very well. He can hit the ball well, too. He is the team's catcher, so he doesn't have to move around so much.

Kacey is one of more than 50,000 physically challenged people in the United States who play sports. These days physically challenged people are doing everything from biking and scuba diving to mountain climbing and rafting. They are dancing and doing martial arts.

Some physically challenged people are great athletes. With hard work and strong wills, they go beyond their physical challenges and make their dreams come true. Sharon Hedrick was the first woman to race the Boston

Sharon Hedrick

Marathon in a wheelchair. She also competed in the 1988 Seoul Olympics. There she won the women's wheelchair 800-meter race in record time.

Diana Golden

Diana Golden became the U.S. Alpine Skier of the Year skiing on one leg. She came in 10th, racing against able-bodied skiers. In 1988 the U.S. Olympic Committee named her Female Skier of the Year over all other racers, including able-bodied skiers.

The Paralympic Games are for physically challenged people. In 1996 Atlanta, Georgia, held the Tenth Paralympic Games right after the summer Olympics. Over 3,000 physically challenged athletes from around the world competed. In Nagano, Japan, 1,000 athletes competed in winter sports at the Paralympic Games in 1998.

Everyone can learn a lot from physically challenged athletes like Kacey, Sharon, and Diana. Kacey says, "Don't let anything get you down. Just play and have fun. Don't let anybody tell you you can't do something. Just say, 'I can!'"

▶ *What did you read?*

Choose another title for the reading.

a. Three Great Athletes   **b.** Special Athletes Work Hard to Win

▶ *Read again*

**Are these sentences true? Find the answers in the reading. Circle *yes* or *no*.
Check your answers with a partner.**

1. Playing basketball is easy for Kacey.	yes	(no)
2. There are 50,000 physically challenged athletes in the world.	yes	no
3. Sharon Hedrick has a strong will and works hard.	yes	no
4. Diana Golden competed in the Olympics.	yes	no
5. Some physically challenged athletes compete against able-bodied athletes.	yes	no
6. The Paralympic Games are for physically challenged people.	yes	no
7. Kacey thinks he can do almost anything.	yes	no

▶ *Talk more about it*

Think about these questions. Then discuss your ideas.

> **1.** Why do you think the coach wouldn't let Kacey play basketball at first? Why did the coach change his mind?
>
> **2.** Kacey says, "Don't let anybody tell you you can't do something. Just say, 'I can!'" What does he mean?

 Physically challenged athletes use 50% more energy in races than able-bodied athletes.

▶ *Write*

A. Look at the mind map and the paragraph below. Notice how the paragraph follows the organization of the mind map.

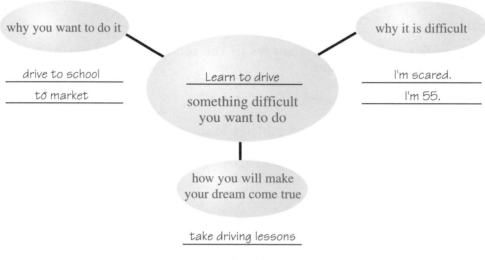

why you want to do it

drive to school
to market

why it is difficult

I'm scared.
I'm 55.

Learn to drive
something difficult
you want to do

how you will make
your dream come true

take driving lessons

I Can!

I want to learn how to drive. I want to drive myself to school and to the market. It's difficult to learn because I am scared. Also, I am 55 years old. Some people say I am too old to learn. Next month I will take driving lessons. I know I can learn.

B. Think about something difficult that you want to do. Fill in the mind map. Then write a paragraph titled "I Can!" on your own paper. Use your mind map and the example to help you.

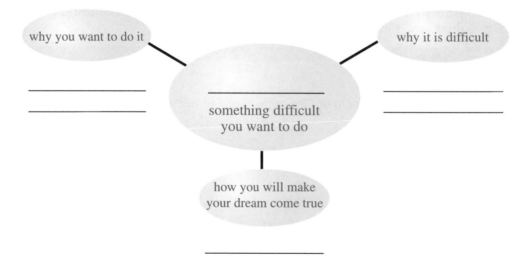

why you want to do it

why it is difficult

something difficult
you want to do

how you will make
your dream come true

Turn to *Remember the Words* at the back of this book.

TEACHER'S NOTES

Teaching the Units

There are three main sections in each unit. TALK ABOUT IT introduces the topic and activates students' prior knowledge of it. READ ABOUT IT and READ MORE ABOUT IT each contain the three components of an effective reading lesson: pre-reading, reading, and post-reading activities.

Before You Read

Teachers can make these pre-reading activities most effective by initially leading the students through them, thereby modeling the strategies a competent reader uses prior to reading a text. The strategies are repeated throughout the book, and teachers can reinforce these strategies by providing other opportunities to use them. New vocabulary is most effectively presented in context. In *Read All About It 2*, most new vocabulary words are evident in the picture captions or the *Before You Read* questions. To help students guess the meaning of the words, teachers may also want to identify other potentially difficult words. It is helpful to write the captions or sentences with unfamiliar words on the board and ask students to guess the meanings. The teacher can point out any clues in the captions, sentences, or pictures that may inform the students' guessing. Modeling this approach to guessing meaning from context is an effective way to accustom students to using the strategy themselves. To avoid overwhelming the students, presenting a maximum of about eight new words is recommended.

While You Read

Since reading is most often a solitary activity, silent reading is an important part of the learning process. Therefore, the readings in this text, with the exception of the poems, are meant to be read individually and silently first. Once students have worked thoroughly with the reading and follow-up exercises, the teacher or students may read the passage aloud to work on pronunciation and to develop fluency in oral reading. The *Read All About It 2* cassette can also be used at this time.

The teacher may want to set a short time limit for reading the passage in *While You Read* and answering the questions in *What did you read?* and *Read again*. A time limit encourages students to rely on context clues for meaning. It also allows all the students to finish reading and answering the *Read again* questions simultaneously, so that they can begin the pair or group work that follows.

Students should be encouraged to guess the meaning of unknown words from context or skip over them as competent readers do. Teachers can point out to students that they will usually be able to grasp the main ideas of the readings and answer the comprehension questions without understanding every word. Students can read for general meaning the first time and refer back to the reading for details during the *Read again* exercises.

Each reading incorporates a number of words from the corresponding unit and other units of *The Oxford Picture Dictionary*, so the readings can be used to reinforce that vocabulary. See page 115 for the Word List with references to *The Oxford Picture Dictionary*.

Although reading the passage and doing *Read again* are intended as individual work, the rest of the activities in *While You Read* are designed for pairs or small groups. Working together gives students the opportunity to negotiate the meaning of the readings and to develop communication skills. During group work, it is helpful to set a time limit and to assign student roles, such as discussion leader, recorder, reporter, or timekeeper, to help the groups run smoothly. Frequently changing pairings or groupings gives students the experience of listening and talking to a variety of speakers.

While communication skills are an important part of the learning process, all exercises can be completed individually if necessary, and most answers can be found in the Answer Key on page 110.

After You Read

In this section reading skills are reinforced through writing and vocabulary activities. New words are often reviewed in *Words, words, words*. Word families are also introduced. When students encounter words they want to learn, they can use the vocabulary diary, *Remember the Words*, at the back of the book. They can also write an original sentence for each word. Vocabulary activities can be done individually in class or used for homework or assessment.

READ MORE ABOUT IT

Since READ MORE ABOUT IT will probably take place in a new class period, teachers may want to conduct a review discussion of the topic. They can rely on students who read the READ ABOUT IT passage for answers to specific review questions. More general questions can be answered by those who did not read that passage. In this way, all students can benefit from the discussion.

Time Frame

Read All About It 2 is easily adaptable to different class situations. Activities can be done in a relatively short period of time or exploited to the fullest extent, depending on the needs and goals of the students and the time available. For example, in TALK ABOUT IT, a teacher could lead students through the activities to shorten the time or have them work in small groups to lengthen it. Teachers can omit any activities that do not suit their objectives.

Units can be easily divided to span more than one class period. Ideally, students would complete TALK ABOUT IT through *Talk more about it* for the first reading in one class. *After You Read* could be done in the next class period or for homework. READ MORE ABOUT IT could be reserved for another class period.

Unit-by-Unit Notes

Procedural Notes (PRO) offer ideas for specific lesson plans and classroom management.

Extension Activities (EXT) are additional reading, writing, or discussion tasks in which students can apply the skills they have learned.

References (REF) list sources of further information for students and teachers. Please note that Internet addresses may change.

Unit 1 Success

Page 1, Talk About It   EXT: Have students share sayings from their countries like "If at first you don't succeed... ."

A Special Teacher

Page 2, Before You Read   PRO: Elicit answers to the questions and write them on the board. Since they are guesses, accept all answers without correcting. After students have read the passage, review the answers on the board and have students identify those predictions that turned out to be true. This procedure can be used in subsequent units.

**Page 3, While You Read   **The students were taking the Advanced Placement Calculus Exam. If they passed, they would receive college credit for high school work.
EXT: This episode is from the 1987 movie *Stand and Deliver*. Show selected video clips and discuss.

Page 4, What did you read?   EXT: Ask students: What were the clues that helped you choose your answer? Use this same question in *What did you read?* in other units.

Page 4, Read again   EXT: If the answer is *no*, have students write the correct answer. Do the same in subsequent lessons.

Page 4, Show you understand   PRO: Demonstrate how to follow the thread of information to find the order. The thread can be a similar word, a different form of the word, or a transition word. Here the thread is: 1. *Mr. Escalante* 2. *He* 3. *So*…teach them *calculus*. 4. …took a *calculus test*. 5. …took the *test* again.

Page 5, Words, words, words   PRO: A. Point out different kinds of context clues, e.g., cognates or roots (Latino/Latin American); restatements ("Some people thought they cheated. They thought they copied the correct answers…"); *or* to set off a definition (a strong desire or wish to learn). Have students use these word attack skills in subsequent units.

A Difficult Beginning

**Page 6, While You Read   **In 1889 Einstein lived in Munich, Germany. At that time the government took over all the schools and instituted military rules and regulations. That may be why Albert, a creative thinker, had "a difficult beginning."

Page 7, Show you understand   EXT: Have students give reasons for their answers orally and in writing.

Page 8, Talk more about it   EXT: Have students write a journal entry about a day in their lives.

Unit 2 Helping Hands

Page 9, Talk About It
REF: http://www.usaweekend.com/diffday/index.html

For the Love of Children

**Page 11, While You Read   **Adoption and physical/mental challenges may be sensitive topics, and some students may be reluctant to discuss personal experiences.
EXT: Review comparative adjectives using examples from the reading, e.g., *busy/busier*.

Page 12, Read again   PRO: This activity requires inferencing. Answers to questions 4, 5, and 6 are not explicitly stated in one sentence in the reading. Reinforce this skill by asking inference questions in subsequent units.

Page 12, Show you understand   EXT: Have students make a similar chart of their daily routines. Point out that they should use the first-person singular, e.g., *I get up*. More advanced students can also write a paragraph.

Page 13, Talk more about it   EXT: Ask students: Do you think there should be special requirements for adopting children? What are they?

The Test, Part 1 and Part 2

Pages 15–18,   PRO: You may wish to split other reading assignments this way to have students practice these comprehension and prediction skills.

The Test, Part 2

Page 17, While You Read   EXT: Review comparative adjectives using examples from the reading, e.g., *old/older, young/younger*.

EXT: Point out that words from nature are used as names e.g., *dawn, lily*. Ask students to think of other names that are nature words. Discuss similar naming practices in students' countries.

EXT: Review superlative adjectives using examples from the reading, e.g., *kind/kindest, helpful/most helpful*.

EXT: Write *said* and *answered* on the board. Elicit other words that can be used and list them. Teach any unfamiliar words. Then have the whole class read Part 1 and ask students to choose appropriate replacements for *said* and *answered*. Students can do the same for Part 2 individually, in pairs, or for homework.

Page 18, What did you read?   EXT: Have students suggest other titles for this story and explain their choices.

Page 18, Talk more about it   EXT: Ask students: Why do many stories like these end with women marrying a prince as a reward? What is the man's reward? Why? How do these stories affect our children?

EXT: Explain that the message of a folktale is called "the moral." Elicit some other folktales and their morals and list them on the board. Discuss cross-cultural similarities.

Unit 3 Home at Last

Hearts and Hands Build Homes

**Page 21, While You Read   **Habitat for Humanity believes that owning a home can be the first step out of poverty. To qualify for a Habitat home, people need an income that is 25–50% of the median income in the area and must be willing to help build it. Building one's own home reduces the cost, increases the family's personal stake in their house, and fosters a sense of community. People are chosen based on: 1. need; 2. ability to pay the non-profit, no interest loan; 3. willingness to help build their home and one other.
EXT: Point out the interchangeable use of the *Deans* and *the Dean family*.
REF: http://www.habitat.org

**Page 22, Show you understand   **See Teacher's Notes for Unit 1, page 106, *Show you understand*, PRO.

Page 22, Talk more about it   EXT: Ask students: Would you like to build your own home? Why or why not?

Page 23, Words, words, words See Teacher's Notes for Unit 1, page 106, *Words, words, words*, PRO.

E-Z Home

Page 24, Before You Read   PRO: A. Skim—Model the activity using a reading from Unit 1 or 2. Give students a short time, e.g., 1 minute, to complete the exercise.

B. Scan—Model the activity using the example. Show students how to run their fingers down the reading to search for the numbers. Give them 2–3 minutes to complete the exercise.

Page 24, While You Read

This type of home was created as low-cost housing. It is intended for gradual expansion so that people can buy what they can afford and not incur a mortgage.

EXT: Point out that x in 15′ x 18′ means "by."

EXT: Review articles using examples from the reading, e.g., *a plumber, an electrician*. Point out that in advertisements, articles are often left out to save space. Have students review an ad and note where articles could be added.

EXT: Show how *house* and *home* are used interchangeably. Have students discuss the differences in meaning.

Page 26, Talk more about it

Some of these homes are used as home offices, units for nannies or family members, vacation cottages, housing for the homeless, or disaster-relief shelters.

EXT: Ask students: Would your friends help you build a house? Why or why not?

Unit 4 Home Cooking

What's Cooking?

Page 29, While you Read   EXT: Make two lists on the board: Cooking verbs on the left and corresponding adjectives on the right, e.g., *v. steam/adj. steamed, fry/fried, barbecue/barbecued, bake/baked, broil/broiled, stir-fry/stir-fried*. Have students guess how to form other adjectives following the examples. Use these verbs: *grill, roast, cook, microwave, boil*. Students can add others to the list.

Page 30, Read again   See Teacher's Notes for Unit 2, page 106, *Read again*, PRO.

REF: http://Food.com and http://www11Webvan.com

Page 30, Talk more about it   EXT:
1. Ask: What are the advantages and disadvantages of buying meals at a convenience store?
2. Have students write a paragraph about either the advantages or disadvantages using the brainstormed lists. Have them title their paragraphs.

Page 31, Words, words, words   EXT: Have students find the other adverb/adjective pair (*fresh/freshly*) in the reading.

Knoxville, Tennessee

Page 32, Before You Read   PRO: Have students find Tennessee on a map (*The Oxford Picture Dictionary*, pages 122–123), and identify the region of the U.S. where it is located. Have them brainstorm anything they know about the South, e.g., climate, people, history, and list their ideas on the board.

Page 33, Read again   EXT: After students complete the chart, point out the compound words in the poem, e.g., *buttermilk, homemade, homecoming, barefooted*. Have the class brainstorm a list of other compound words they know.

Page 33, Talk more about it   EXT: Have students draw a picture of the scene they imagine from reading the poem. In small groups, have them show their pictures and talk about them. Volunteers can discuss their pictures with the class.

Page 34, Write   PRO:
1. Model this activity. Copy the poem format from page 34 on the board. Then, answer the first question by telling the class your favorite season and writing it the appropriate place. (Numbers of spaces correspond to question numbers. Numbers can be added or deleted to make the poem longer or shorter.) Continue answering the questions and asking students where to write the answers.
2. Have students work in pairs to write a poem. They can write a simple one and embellish it later with adjectives and details. Have them write titles for their poems.

EXT: After completing their poems, have students practice making the phrases into sentences, but note that the result is no longer a poem.

REF: Kazemek, Francis E. and Pat Rigg, *Enriching Our Lives: Poetry Lessons for Adult Literacy Teachers and Tutors*, International Reading Association, 1995.

Unit 5 Fashion Statements

Page 35, Talk About It   PRO: A. Demonstrate how to find information in a graph. Use question 1 as an example.
B. Model how to rate in question 3. Explain your reasoning.

Dressing Down

Page 36, Before You Read

PRO: See Teacher's Notes for Unit 3, page 107, *Before you read*, PRO B.

Page 37, While You Read   PRO:
1. Explain that one meaning of *dressing down* is to dress casually, the opposite of *dressing up*.
2. Explain that *memo* is an abbreviation for *memorandum*, an informal written communication in an office.

EXT: Review comparative adjectives using examples from the reading, e.g., *more comfortable, better*.

Page 39, Brainstorm and write   PRO: Review adverbs of frequency *always, usually, sometimes*, and *never* before doing this activity. Refer to the graph in *Talk About It*, page 35.

Coolhunters

Page 40, While You Read   EXT: Review superlative adjectives using examples from the reading, e.g., coolest.

Unit 6 To Your Health

Page 43, Talk About It   PRO:
1. Emphasize that this is a speaking/listening activity, so students should interview as many people as possible. Give a time limit. To faciliate this activity, students should have their own books with them. They should also ask interviewees how to spell their names if necessary.
2. Elicit answers to questions, e.g., Who gets exercise every day? Write all the names on the board next to the number of the item. Use the information to ask questions, e.g., Does Juan get eight hours of sleep? Does Yoko or Maria exercise every day? How many students get acupuncture?

No More Pain

Page 45, While You Read   While traveling with former President Nixon in China in 1972, James Reston, a U.S. foreign correspondent, needed surgery. It was performed with acupuncture to stop the pain. Reston was so impressed with the effectiveness of acupuncture that he introduced it to the U.S. in various articles and TV programs. Although acupuncture had been used for years by Chinese people, this is how it first became well known to Americans.

EXT: Many names for health practitioners end in *–ist*, e.g., *acupuncturist, cardiologist.* Ask students to name others.

EXT: Ask students: Some people go to acupuncturists, chiropractors *and* medical doctors. Why?

REF: http://www.acupuncture.com/

An Apple a Day

Page 48, While You Read

EXT: Have students share health-related sayings from their countries like "An apple a day keeps the doctor away" and "Feed a cold, starve a fever."

EXT: "You're pulling my leg" means "You're joking." The equivalent Spanish expression is "You're pulling my hair." Have students generate body-related idioms from their countries.

REF:
http://www.healthcentral.com/news/newsfulltext.cfm?id=3285

Unit 7 Emergency Action

Page 51, Talk About It   EXT: A. Bring in headlines from the newspaper and ask students to predict the content of the articles. B. Ask students to name what other things should/can be done in case of emergency.

Friends in Need

Pages 52–53, While You Read   Some stores were probably not accepting credit cards because computers were down, and checks and credit cards couldn't be electronically verified.

EXT: Ask students: Which paragraph goes with which picture in the story? How do you know?

EXT: Point out that the title comes from the saying "A friend in need is a friend indeed." Remind students of the sayings in Unit 6 (See Teacher's Notes, page 108, *While You Read,* EXT.) Elicit sayings about friendship from the students' countries.

EXT: Have students find the area on a map of North America (See *The Oxford Picture Dictionary,* pages 122-123).

Page 54, Talk more about it   During this storm people cooked on barbecues and over campfires. They used generators for electric stoves and heaters. To keep warm, some people slept in several layers of clothing, with many people in one room. Others lit fires in fireplaces or had bonfires outside.

EXT: Ask students: What questions do you think Marie Dupont and the other driver asked each other before they borrowed each other's car?

Page 55, Words, words, words   EXT: Ask students to find another adjective in the reading that ends in *y* (*needy*).

Page 55, Brainstorm and write   Examples are from the reading. Answers will vary depending on the specific emergency.

El Niño

Pages 56–57, While You Read   In Spanish *El Niño* means "the little boy." It is also used to refer to the Christ child. The Peruvian fisherman called the warm water El Niño because it came in December like the Christ child. *La Niña* means "the little girl" in Spanish.

EXT: Have students locate the place names in the reading (See *The Oxford Picture Dictionary,* pages 122–125).

EXT: Review comparative and superlative adjectives using examples from the reading, e.g., *cold/colder, big/biggest.*

REF: El Niño: http://www.pmel.noaa.gov/toga-tao/el-nino-story.html
La Niña: http://www.pmel.noaa.gov/toga-tao/la-nina-story.html

Unit 8 Getting There

**Page 59, Talk About It   **A. A different kind of transportation should be listed in each circle. Add more circles to extend the activity. Note that *on foot* can also be included.

Traveling Through Time

Page 60, Before You Read   PRO: Skim/Scan—See Teacher's Notes for Unit 3, page 107, *Before You Read,* PRO, A and B.

Pages 60–61, While You Read   These letters show different types of transportation used in traveling from San Francisco to Los Angeles, CA from the perspectives of three different family members: William, the grandfather, (1925); Bill, the father, (1975); and a futuristic view from Bill's daughter, Willa, (2025).

Bill and Will are nicknames for men named William. Willa is a female derivation. Point out that people in the U.S. often name children after a family member.

PRO: These letters could be used as a three-person jigsaw. For information on technique, see Teacher's Notes, Unit 10, page 109, READ MORE ABOUT IT. For specific directions, see shaded boxes in the text on pages 82–86.

EXT: In 1925 a new car cost about $500 in the U.S. Ask students: How much does it cost to buy a new car now in the U.S.? In your country?

REF: high speed trains:
http://eb-p5.eb.uah.edu/maglev/maglev.html
smart cars: see *Odyssey Magazine,* May 1998, vol. 7, iss. 5.

Unit 9 Women Make History

**Page 67, Talk About It   **A. When this riddle originally circulated in the 1950s, almost all U.S. doctors were men. Although now there are many women doctors in the U.S., the majority are men, so this riddle might still be difficult for Americans to solve. For students from countries where women doctors are common, the riddle might be easier.

A Woman's Place

Page 68, Before You Read   PRO: Scan—See Teacher's Notes for Unit 3, page 107, *Before You Read,* PRO B.

Page 71, Outline   PRO: Explain that the purpose of an outline is to list the main ideas and details of a reading passage, and that an outline can be helpful in studying information. Have students read the details listed under each blank and match a main idea. To practice, have students identify the main ideas and details of other readings while you write an outline on the board.

Encyclopedia of Women in Science

Page 73, Before You Read   PRO: Review the types of readings students have encountered in other units, e.g., magazine and newspaper articles, folktales, etc. Ask students to name other types of readings they know. Then have them answer the questions.

Page 73-74, While You Read To replicate the style of an encyclopedia, these passages have more difficult vocabulary than any others. Students are not expected to understand every word. Their task is to get the basic information.

PRO: Explain that when we use an encyclopedia, we select things to read according to our interest. Have students look at the pictures and the captions to help them decide which two women to read about. Tell them they will have a chance to read about the other women later. Mention: 1. NASA stands for National Aeronautics and Space Administration; 2. the National Institutes of Health is often referred to as NIH.

EXT: Review the nouns in the article that denote an area of study and the person who studies it, e.g., *astronomy/astronomer*; *physics/physicist*; *science/scientist*.

EXT: Review comparative adjectives using examples from the reading, e.g., *safe/safer, clean/cleaner*.

Page 75, Read again   PRO: Students should answer the questions on their own. Tell them that in the next activity they will be sharing the information with their classmates.

Page 76, Show you understand   This is an information gap activity. Some students have information that other students don't have. The purpose is to exchange information through real communication.

PRO: Emphasize that this is a listening/speaking activity. Each student needs to find another student who read about a different woman. The student asks questions and fills in the chart for that woman. Then students change partners and follow the same procedure until their charts are completed. Students can check their work with a partner. As a whole-class activity, elicit the important things each woman did and write them on the board.

Page 76, Write   Explain that a mind map can be used to organize information and help students write. Here students make a mind map to record the main ideas and details in a reading.

Unit 10 Puzzling Plants
Kudzu

Pages 78–79, While You Read   EXT: Review the use of the possessive apostrophe as in *Sanders'* and *Tim's*.
REF: http://www.cptr.ua.edu/kudzu/

Page 81, Write an outline   PRO: See Teacher's Notes for Unit 9, page 108, *Outline*, PRO. In this activity, have students read the main ideas (I–IV) and review why the details listed fit into each section. Then have them fill in the blanks.

EXT: Have students use the outline to help retell the story to a partner. They can add any other details they remember.

Pages 82–86, Read More About It   These readings are a *jigsaw*, an activity in which some students read one reading and other students read another. Jigsaws encourage authentic communication by giving students a reason to read and exchange information. Teachers who prefer not to use the jigsaw format can have all students complete the readings and activities in the order they appear.

PRO: Follow the instructions in the lesson for grouping students in teams of 4. Assign any extra students to groups, but no group should have more than 5 people. The extra person in each group is a number 1. The two number 1s in those groups will work together. All the 1s and 2s move to one side of the room, and all the 3s and 4s move to the other side to do *While You Read, What did you read?, Read again*, and *Show you*

understand, Part A, so they can discuss the activities without being overheard by their other team members. Tell students that they will eventually read both stories. For *Show you understand*, Part B, students can return to their original seats with their team.

Pages 84, 86, Show you understand   PRO: B. In Part A students fill in the chart for the story they read. In B they take a new partner, turn to the chart for the story that partner read, ask their partner questions, and fill in the chart. Emphasize that this is a listening/speaking activity. They should not read their partner's story or look at their partner's chart.

Pages 84, 86, Read more   After the students read the other story they can complete the corresponding *Read again*.

EXT: Ask students: Why do people tell folktales? Give two reasons. Do you know any folktales from your country? Tell one.

Unit 11 Good Work
Page 87, Talk About It   PRO: Explain any difficult job titles.

Work for the Future
Page 88, Before You Read   PRO: Scan—See Teacher's Notes for Unit 3, page 107, *Before You Read*, PRO B.

Page 88–89, While You Read   "Baby boomer" is the nickname for the generation featured in this reading.
EXT: Review comparative adjectives using examples from the reading, e.g., *old/older, young/younger*.

Page 91, Words, words, words   PRO: See Teacher's Notes for Unit 1, page 106, *Words, words, words*.
REF: http://sunsentinel.webpoint.com/job/yourjob.htm

Make It Your Business
Page 92–93, While You Read
REF: http://www.greenglass.com/legend.html

Page 94, Write   PRO: The purpose is to get students thinking about how they might start their own businesses by turning something they like doing for recreation into a business.

Unit 12 Dare To Dream
Dream Adventures

Pages 97–98, While You Read   PRO: Jigsaw reading. See Teacher's Notes for Unit 10, page 109, READ MORE ABOUT IT.
REF: http://www.fodors.com/sports/

I Can!
Pages 101–102, While You Read
REF:
http://www.olympic-usa.org/games/ga_2_2_1_1.html

Page 104, Write   PRO: Explain that a mind map is a brainstorming tool used in the writing process. In Part B, have students fill in something difficult they want to do. Then have them write responses to the other prompts. They can add more lines if necessary. Once the mind map is complete, students can use the information to write their paragraphs. Students should add a concluding sentence.

ANSWER KEY

Please note: Answers are not given for prediction or opinion answers.

Unit 1

Talk About It [page 1]

A. 1. b   2. b   3. b

A Special Teacher

What did you read? [page 4]   b

Read again [page 4]

1. no   2. yes   3. yes   4. yes   5. no   6. no   7. yes

Show you understand [page 4]

1. b   2. e   3. c   4. d   5. a

Words, words, words [page 5]

A. 1. d   They didn't have much money.

2. a   They spoke Spanish at home.

3. c   …or wish to learn.

4. e   …did well… What a success!

5. b   …copied the correct answers from other students' papers.

B. Arturo Soriano wants to be a **successful** artist. He will **succeed** because he is studying hard. His **success** will make his family proud.

A Difficult Beginning

What did you read? [page 7]   b

Read again [page 7]

1. evening	morning	4. spoke	apologized
2. soft	hard	5. foggy	cloudy
3. closed	opened	6. read	discuss

Unit 2

Talk About It [page 9]

Students and teachers will repair public schools. Volunteers will clean parks. Children will bake bread for the elderly. Teenagers will collect money to buy toys for needy children.

For the Love of Children

What did you read? [page 12]   a

Read again [page 12]

A. 1. yes   2. yes   3. yes   4. no   5. no   6. yes

B. 4. Camille is very busy … she has help…

5. Camille makes their breakfast. …Camille cooks dinner. She sometimes cooks for 30 people…

6. Together they wake up, bathe, and dress the children. …Mike cleans up the kitchen…

Show you understand [page 12]

5:00 a.m.	gets up greets helpers
5:00–6:00 a.m.	wakes up, bathes, and dresses children
6:00–7:30 a.m.	makes and serves breakfast
7:30–9:30 a.m.	naps
9:30 a.m.–noon	does laundry
noon–1:00 p.m.	makes and serves lunch
1:00–5:00 p.m.	swims, exercises, plays with children, gives physical therapy, goes to the market
5:00–7:00 p.m.	makes and serves dinner
7:00–10:00 p.m.	helps Renae and Jaclyn do their homework
midnight	goes to bed

Words, words, words [page 13]

A. 1. c   2. d   3. b   4. e   5. a

B. Mike and Camille have three adult **helpers**. They also **help** each other. Their daughters are **helpful**, too.

The Test, Part 1

Read again [page 16]

1. yes   2. no   3. no   4. yes   5. no   6. yes

Before You Read [page 16]

A. 1. She was lazy.

2. They visited the king.

3. No. (*Answers will vary.*)

The Test, Part 2

Read again [page 18]

1. b   2. a   3. b   4. b   5. a   6. a

What did you read? [page 18]   a

Unit 3

Talk About It [page 19]

A. 1. 2 bedrooms, 1 bathroom

2. (*Answers will vary.*)

3. (*Answers will vary.*)

Hearts and Hands Build Homes

What did you read? [page 22]   a

Read again [page 22]

1. yes   2. no   3. yes   4. no   5. no   6. yes   7. no

Show you understand [page 22]

1. c   2. e   3. g   4. b   5 a   6. f   7. d

Pronouns [page 23]

1. They → several people

2. they → volunteers

3. It → the old building

4. we → My family and I

5. he → Peter

6. she → Kathy

Words, words, words [page 23]

1. d nearby

2. c all over the world

3. a give their time

4. b plant some bushes and flowers

Before You Read [page 24]

A. 3

B. 1. b 2. d 3. a 4. e 5. c

E-Z Home

What did you read? [page 26]

A small house can be all you need.

Read again [page 26]

1. b 2. a 3. b 4. b 5. b 6. a

Show you understand [page 26]

E-Z Home is **small**, but it has everything you need. It has a living area, a **kitchen**, a sleeping area, a **dining** area, and a bathroom. All you need is a **screwdriver** and a wrench to put the house together, and you can **build** your house in about a week. When you need more **space**, you can add a **bedroom** or a family room.

Unit 4

Talk About It [page 27]

A. 1. No. Alexander left to play tennis. Cookie went to a movie.

2. No. There's practically nothing to eat in the house.

3. (*Answers will vary.*)

4. (*Answers will vary.*)

What's Cooking?

What did you read? [page 30]   b

Read again [page 30]

A. 1. no 2. yes 3. no 4. yes 5. yes 6. yes

B. 2. Most of us are in a hurry…

5. People can get to these stores easily and shop quickly.

6. If you are too busy to cook … use your computer … Your dinner can be ready in an hour.

Words, words, words [page 31]

A. 1. e 2. b 3. f 4. d 5. c 6. g 7. a

B. It's **easy** to buy healthy meals at Michael's Market. You can buy delicious, fresh food there. And it's **quick**. You can get there *easily* and buy your meal *quickly*.

Knoxville, Tennessee

What did you read? [page 33]   b

Read again [page 33]

What does she like to eat?	Where does she like to go?	What does she like to do?
fresh corn	church picnic	eat
okra	church homecoming	listen to gospel music
cabbage	the mountains	go barefoot
barbecue		
buttermilk		
ice cream		

Unit 5

Talk About It [page 35]

A. 1. a 2. b 3. a 4. a 5. a

Before You Read [page 36]

B. 1. a or b 2. b

Dressing Down

What did you read? [page 38]

Many office workers wear casual clothing to **work**.

Read again [page 38]

1. yes 2. no 3. no 4. yes 5. yes 6. no 7. yes

Show you understand [page 38]

Women: pants, sweaters, knit shirts
Men: casual pants, sports shirts, knit shirts, sports coat, sweaters

Coolhunters

What did you read? [page 41]

Fashion designers get ideas from cool kids.

Read again [page 42]

1. yes 2. yes 3. no 4. no 5. yes 6. no 7. no

Show you understand [page 42]

Baysie and Deedee **hunt** for cool kids. They find them in small **clothing** stores or on the **street**. Baysie and Deedee talk to the kids and take **pictures** of their clothing. They want to **find** the next **cool** fashion.

Unit 6

No More Pain

What did you read? [page 45]   b

Read again [page 46]

1. a   2. b   3. a   4. b   5. a   6. b

Show you understand [page 46]

1. yes   That made me feel a little better...

2. yes   ...the needles make him feel better ... My pain is almost gone.

3. no   He also looks at what Daniel eats. He studies Daniel's thoughts and feelings, too.

4. no   In China people have used acupuncture for thousands of years. It has been common in Korea and Japan for centuries.

5. yes   more than 4,000 medical doctors use acupuncture ... Some doctors ... are sending their patients ... to acupuncturists

6. yes   ...health insurance companies are paying for acupuncture...

Words, words, words [page 47]

A. 1. c   2. d   3. a   4. b   5. e

B. Acupuncture has become very popular. Acupuncturists **treat** people for pain and illnesses. Studies show that the **treatments** work.

An Apple a Day

What did you read? [page 49]   a

Read again [page 49]

Food	Disease
all kinds of fruits and vegetables	lung, colon, and stomach cancer
spinach	breast cancer, heart disease
yellow corn	breast cancer, heart disease
grapes	allergies, heart attacks, strokes
garlic	colds, flu, cancer
soybeans	osteoporosis, breast cancer
cranberry juice	bladder infections

Words, words, words [page 50]

1. fight → prevent, cut the chances of getting

2. cancer → heart disease, strokes, osteoporosis

3. corn → spinach, broccoli, garlic

4. apples → oranges, grapes, mangoes, watermelon

5. red → yellow, green, orange

Unit 7

Talk About It [page 51]

A. 1. b   2. c   3. d   4. a

B. Listen to the radio 1,2,3

   Use flashlights 2

   Keep refrigerator closed 2

   Use other roads 1,3

   Build a fire 2

   Move things off the floor 3

   Contact family members 1,2,3

   Fill containers with clean drinking water 3

Friends in Need

What did you read? [page 54]   b

Read again [page 54]

1. no   2. yes   3. no   4. no   5. yes   6. no   7. yes
8. yes   9. no

Show you understand [page 54]

What was closed?	What stayed open?	Who helped others?
schools	markets	hotel
stores	fire stations	health club
businesses	hotel	families
post office	health club	firefighters
subway station		army/soldiers

Words, words, words [page 55]

A. 1. c   2. b   3. d   4. a   5. f   6. e

B. During the storm the **icy** streets made travel difficult. The **ice** on the trees was heavy and made the branches crack.

El Niño

What did you read? [page 57]   b

Read again [page 58]

1. no   2. no   3. no   4. yes   5. no   6. yes   7. yes

Show you understand [page 58]

Brazil	drought
Canada	ice storm, warm winter weather
China	floods
Ecuador	floods
Indonesia	drought
Mexico	snow, high coastal waves
Peru	mudslides
Philippines	drought
Somalia	floods
United States	ice storm, tornadoes, mudslides, blizzard

Unit 8

Before You Read [page 60]

A. 3

B. 1. 1925, 1975, 2025   2. William, Bill, Willa

Traveling Through Time

What did you read? [page 62]   b

Read again [page 62]

	Reading 1	Reading 2	Reading 3
1.	train	subway, plane, taxi	sports car
2.	14 hours	1 hour	5 1/2 hours
3.	7:00 a.m.	10:00 a.m.	1:00 p.m.
4.	business trip	business lunch	business meeting

Show you understand [page 62]

William, Bill, and Willa wrote letters to their **friends**. They wanted to **invite** them out to eat. They also wanted to tell them about their **trips** to Los Angeles. Bill also needed to **apologize** to his friend because he canceled their lunch date.

The three writers are in the same family. William is Bill's **father** and Willa's **grandfather**.

Find the reason [page 63]

1. c   2. f   3. a   4. e   5. b   6. d

Get Out of Your Car!

What did you read? [page 66]   a

Read again [page 66]

1. no   2. yes   3. yes   4. no   5. no   6. yes   7. yes

Unit 9

Talk About It [page 67]

A. the boy's mother

Before You Read [page 68]

B. 1776, 1830, 1860, 1861, 1920, 1945, 1949, 1981

A Woman's Place

What did you read? [page 70]   b

Read again [page 70]

1. no   2. no   3. yes   4. doesn't say   5. doesn't say
6. yes   7. no   8. no

Show you understand [page 70]

1776 → b	1920 → f
1830 → d	1945 → e
1861 → a	Today → c

Outline [page 71]

I. In 1776 women did not have many rights.

II. Things began to change.

III. Today women have equal rights.

Puzzle [page 72]

1. vote
2. rights
3. century
4. fight

5. owned
6. managers
7. pay

secret word: victory

Before You Read [page 73]

1. 7   2. (*Answers will vary.*)

Encyclopedia of Women in Science

What did you read? [page 75]

There are many great women scientists.

Read again [page 75]

(*Answers may vary somewhat.*)

Scientist/Her job/Two important things she did

1. Dr. Gertrude Belle Elion/biochemist/She developed medications for cancer. She also won the Nobel Prize in medicine.

2. Dr. Mae C. Jemison/astronaut, doctor/She became the first female African-American astronaut. She has been a professor at Dartmouth College.

3. Dr. Maria Goeppert Mayer/physicist/She made important discoveries about the structure of atoms. She won the Nobel Prize in physics.

4. Maria Mitchell/astronomer/She discovered a new comet. She was the first woman elected to the Academy of Arts and Sciences.

5. Dr. Antonia Novello/Surgeon General, pediatrician/She studied how AIDS hurt women and their babies. She became the first woman and first Hispanic Surgeon General of the U.S.

6. Dr. Ellen Swallow Richards/chemist/She called the study of the environment *ecology*. She developed *home economics*.

7. Dr. Chien-Shiung Wu/physicist/She helped develop the first atomic bomb. She became a professor of physics at Columbia University.

Unit 10
Kudzu

What did you read? [page 79]   a

Read again [page 80]

1. six months

2. He saw a large hill of vines and cut them away with an ax.

3. Japan and China

4. 200 pounds

5. 1876

6. caterpillar, other insects from China

Show you understand [page 80]

1. d   2. c   3. f   4. a   5. b   6. e

Words, words, words [page 81]

1. e   2. d   3. b   4. a   5. f   6. c

Write an outline [page 81]

I.   A. native to Japan, China
     C. grows one foot a day

II. B. feeds animals

III. C. kills forests

IV. A. scientists tried poisons

The Real Flower
While You Read [page 83]
A bee flew in the open window and went to the real flower.

What did you read? [page 83]   a
Read again [page 84]
1. yes   2. no   3. doesn't say   4. yes
5. no   6. no   7. yes   8. yes

Show you understand [page 84]
A. 1. Queen Leyla, King Aba, artists
   2. At Queen Leyla's palace
   3. He needs to find the real flower.

The Witch and the Rosebushes
While You Read [page 85]
Since the woman was not a rosebush at night, her rosebush did not have dew in the morning. The husband cut the flower from the bush that had no dew.

What did you read? [page 85]   b
Read again [page 86]
1. a 2. b 3. b · 4. b 5. a 6. b 7. a

Show you understand [page 86]
A. 1. the witch, the woman, the husband, the son, and the king
   2. In a village…
   3. He needs to find out which rosebush is his wife.

Unit 11
Before You Read [page 88]
A. b
B. Travel and Hospitality, Finance, Health Care, Nutrition and Fitness, Sales

Work for the Future
What did you read? [page 89]   a
Read again [page 90]
1. yes 2. yes 3. yes 4. no 5. yes 6. no 7. yes

Show you understand [page 90]
1. c 2. d 3. b 4. e 5. f 6. a

Words, words, words [page 91]
A. 1. f 2. a 3. b 4. e 5. d 6. c
B. My mom is going to **retire** soon. She's planning to relax, play golf, and travel during her **retirement**. She's really looking forward to it.

Make It Your Business
What did you read? [page 93]
Simple ideas can often make successful businesses.

Read again [page 94]
1. b 2. b 3. b 4. a 5. b 6. b 7. b

Unit 12
Dream Adventures, Scuba Diving and Dream Adventures, Backpacking
What did you read? [page 99]
People can do many exciting things for recreation.

Read again [page 99]
1. yes 2. yes 3. no 4. no 5. yes 6. yes

Show you understand [page 99]

	Scuba Diving	Backpacking
1.	Costa Rica	Canadian Rockies
2.	4 days	7 days
3.	manta rays, white-tip sharks, fish	wild animals, moose, bighorn sheep, big birds, bald eagles
4.	underwater caves	high waterfalls, rushing rivers, mountain peaks, lakes, forests
5.	4	15
6.	$395	$475
7.	diving mask, snorkel, fins, wet suit, scuba tank	tents, camping stoves, lanterns

Puzzle [page 100]
1. adventure
2. guide
3. clear
4. exploring
5. certified
6. rushing
7. famous

I Can!
What did you read? [page 103]   b
Read again [page 103]
1. no 2. no 3. yes 4. yes 5. yes 6. yes 7. yes

WORD LIST

Here are the words from *Read All About It 2* that are in *The Oxford Picture Dictionary*. To find a word in this list, look for the title of the reading where you saw the word, and then find the word under the title. The first number after each word refers to the page in *The Oxford Picture Dictionary* where you can find the word. The second number (or letter) refers to the item on that page.

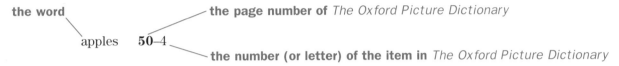

the word

apples   **50**–4

the page number of *The Oxford Picture Dictionary*

the number (or letter) of the item in *The Oxford Picture Dictionary*

If only the **bold** page number appears, that word is part of the unit title or subtitle or is somewhere else on the page.

The words in the list are in the form you see in the reading. When the word in the list has a very different form from the word in the *Dictionary*, you will see the *Dictionary* word next to it (**copied**   copy   **6**–F). When the word in the reading is used as a different part of speech from the word in the *Dictionary*, the part of speech appears after the word in the list.

n. = noun;   *v.* = verb;   *adv.* = adverb;   *adj.* = adjective

Words in the list that are in **bold** type are verbs or verb phrases.

Unit 1 Success
A Special Teacher, p. 3
answers (see **circle** the answer) **7**-S
apples **50**-4
calculus **118**-28
chef's *adj.* **63**-11
class (see a classroom) **2**-3
copied copy 6-F
cooking *n.* **cook 140**-C
correct *adj.* (see **correct** the mistake) **7**-Z
cutting (see **cut up**) **58**-M
desk **142**-1
difficult **11**-24
eighths one-eighth **15**-1
every day **18**-21
families family **24**-25
fourths one-fourth **15**-2
fractions **15**
gave give 21-D
hat **66**-1
helped 6-J
high school **112**-7
home (see places to live) **34**
in front of **13**-4
knife **59**-12, 16
learn, learning *n.* **28**-E
math problems (see mathematics) **118**
money **20**
mornings **17**-16
papers (see **pass out** the papers) **7**-O
Saturday **18**-7
school **5**
shopping **21**
spoke speak 140-J
sports **158-160**
spring **19**-37

stood (see **stand up**) **2**-D
students **2**-3
studied, study *v.* studying **6-7**
take...test **116**-C
teach, teaching *v.* (see teacher) **5**-2
teacher **5**-2
teenagers **22**-6
thirds one-third **15**-3
3% **15** (7-11)
took...test **take**...test **116**-C
United States **122-125**
Wednesdays **18**-4
whole **15**-6
year **18**-8

A Difficult Beginning, p. 6
angry **31**-29
answers...question **6**-H
apologized 8-I
asked, asking *n.* **ask 6**-G
began begin 8-B
chairs **2**-7
chalkboard **2**-1
class (see a classroom) **2**-3
classroom **2**-3
cloudy **10**-7
discuss 6-L
evenings **17**-19
Friday **18**-6
frustrated **31**-28
gray **12**-5
greeted 8-A
hard **11**-5
heard hear 75-B
home (see places to live) **34**
house **34**-6
inventions **114-115**
listen 2-C

man **22**-11
math problems (see mathematics) **118**
minutes **16**-2
morning **17**-16
music **120**
new **71**-32
number **14**
on **13**-8
opened...books **2**-I
parents **24**-4
party (see a graduation) **33**
physics **119**-3
play 120-A
quiet **11**-12
rain *v.* **raining 10**-8
raised...hand **2**-A
read 6-B
sat down sit down 2-E
school **5**
stood up stand up 2-D
studied *v.*, study studying **6-7**
talk 7-P
talking *n.* **talk 7**-P
teacher **5**-2
telephone **9**-1
thick **11**-7
uncomfortable **30**-8
walked 101-A
world **124-125**
write 2-G
wrote write 2-G

Unit 2 Helping Hands
For the Love of Children, p. 11
adult **22**-9
babies **22**-2
baby food **95**-28

bathe 76-B
begins 8-B
bought a house buy a house 29-O
breakfast 61
buys 21-C
cars 106
children 22-1
cleans up (see clean the house) 27-N
comes home 27-Q
cooks dinner 27-P
daughters 24-21
day 18-10
do...homework 27-T
does...laundry 72
dress 94-J
drove drive 26-I
every day 18-21
exercise 27-W
expensive 11-19
family 24-25
food (see food preparation) 58
gallons 57-5
get up 26-B
go to bed 27-X
goes to the market 26-L
goes to work 26-I
good 11-17
got married get married 28-L
greet 8-A
happy 31-32
have dinner 27-R
help n. help 6-J
helps 6-J
hospital 88-7
hours 16-3
jars 56-2
kitchen 40
life (see life events) 28-29
love (see in love) 30-19
lunch 61
makes 26-F
midnight 17-21
milk 54-35
naps (see take a nap) 94-L
night 17-20
nurse 84-10
pediatrician 86-4
physical therapy (see physical
    therapist) 81-30
physically challenged 22-25
play 94-K
pool (see swimming pool) 37-16
proud 31-22
swim 157-T
take care of...the children 140-L
take...the children to school 26-G
takes a nap 94-L
teenagers 22-6
tired 31-33
toddlers 22-3
twice a week 18-23
wake up...the children 26-A
wakes up 26-A
working work 26-K

The Test, pp. 15, 17
afternoon 17-18
angry 31-29
answered 6-H
arrived 111-O

ask, asked 6-G
beard 23-6
beautiful 11-21
began begin 8-B
boy 22-4
breakfast 61
clothes (see clothing) 64-65
crying adj. cry 32-C
cup 63-21
daughters 24-21
day 18-10
dirty 72-15
disgusted 30-9
early 17-22
eat 60-A
embarrassed 31-25
family 24-25
far from 13
father 24-6
flower 129-7
food (see food preparation) 58
garden (see a yard) 39
gave give 21-D
get up 26-B
got dressed get dressed 26-D
got married get married 28-L
hair 23
happy 31-32
help, helped, help n. 6-J
housekeeper 138-33
hungry 30-5
in 13-5
interview (see go on an interview) 141-H
interviewing (see go on an interview)
    141-H
invited 169-B
leave 111-L
lily 129-24
line 55-20
little 11-1
live, lived 116-B
long 23-3
made make 26-F
man 22-11
messy 11-16
morning 17-16
named v. name 4-1
old (see elderly 22-15)
one o'clock 16-4
orange 50-10
parents 24-4
proud 31-22
ran run 156-C
sad 31-20
said say 6-C
secretary 142-3
sister 24-8
sleepy 30-3
small village (see a small town) 34-3
spoke speak (see talk) 7-P
walk, walking 101-A
was born be born 28-A
water 57-1
went to work go to work 26-I
wife 24-20
woke up wake up 26-A
woman 22-10
young 22-13

Unit 3 Home at Last
*Hearts and Hands Build
    Homes, p. 21*
apartment 34-5
backyard 38-2
bathroom 43
beautiful 11-21
bedrooms 44
broken 49-15
build, building (see construction) 149
building (see apartment building) 34-5
bushes 39-20
business people (see businessman/
    businesswoman) 136-10
cabinets 40-1
carpenters 48-12
children 22-1
community (see city streets) 88-89
dining area 41
electricians 48-9
excited 31-23
families family 24-25
fence 38-3
floor plan 38-1
floors 44-24
flowers 39-19
furnace is...broken 49-15
garage 38-6
get a loan 35-I
help 6-J
high school 112-7
home (see house) 34-6
hours 16-3
house 34-6
kitchen 40
landlord 37-32
leaks (see ...is leaking) 48-3
light fixtures 41-5
living live 116-B
living room 42
manager 143-25
morning 17-16
nearby (see near) 13
next to 13-1
new 71-32
old 71-33
pay 21-C
pay...mortgage 35-L
place to live 34
plant 39-D
roof 38-20
roofers 48-8
said say 6-C
Saturday 18-7
standing stand (see stand up) 2-D
street 90-9
students 2-3
sunny 10-6
today 18-15
walls are cracked 48-4
work 26-K
world 124-125
volunteers 87-19
yard 39

E-Z Home, p. 24
architect 136-4
ask 6-G
bathroom 43

week **18**-11
world **124-125**

Unit 6 To Your Health
No More Pain, p. 45

Unit 7 Emergency Action
Friends in Need, p. 52

money **20**
months **18**-9
music **120**
near **13**
night **17**-20
occupation **136-139**
one-half **15**-4
one-third **15**-3
parties party **169**
party **169**
playing *n.* **play 120**-A
problem (see difficult problem) **11**-24
professor (see teacher) **5**-2
recycled *adj.* **recycle 126**-A
retirement *n.* **retire 29**
sad **31**-20
salesclerks **139**-50
school **112**
school dances (see a graduation) **33**
shapes **118**
South Africa **124-125**
speakers **164**-11
small (see little) **11**-1
student **2**-3
study *v.* studying **6-7**
today **18**-15
two-thirds **15**
United States **122-125**
university **112**-10
vases **41**-9
weddings (see **get married**) **28**-L
wine glass **63**-20
workers (see jobs and occupations)
    136-139
working *n.* **work 26**-K
world **124-125**
year **18**-8
young **22**-13

Unit 12 Dare to Dream
Dream Adventures, Scuba Diving, p. 97

adventure (see adventure story) **166**-13
backpacking **154**-7
biking **159**-4
call 141-E
canoeing **154**-3
canyon **117**-17
Costa Rica **124-125**
costs *v.* cost **21**-6
days **18**-10
diving mask **155**-3
exploring (see exploration) **114**
fax 142-B
fins **155**-2
fish **130**
fishing **154**-6
hike *v.* hiking **154**-6
hiking **154**-6
instructor **139**-58
jump 156-J
learn (see **learn** to drive) **28**-E
learn to drive **28**-E
manta rays (see ray) **130**-6
million **14**
ocean **155**-1
physically challenged **22**-25
plane (see airplane) **110**-9
price **21**-2,3,6
race car (see sports car) **106**-6

sailboarding **160**-10
schools **112**
scuba dive *v.* scuba diving **160**-12
scuba divers (see scuba diving) **160**-12
scuba tank **155**-8
see 75-A
ski *adj.* skiing **160**-1, 3
skiing **160**-1, 3
snorkel (see snorkeling) **160**-11
students **139**-57
swimming *n.* **swim 157**-T
tennis **159**-14
today **18**-15
warm **10**-2
waters **155**-1
week **18**-11
wet suit **155**-7
white-tip sharks (see shark) **130**-7
world **124-125**

Dream Adventures, Backpacking, p. 98

adventure (see adventure story)
    166-13
animals (see mammals) **134-135**
August **19**-32
backpacking **154**-7
backpacks **154**-15
bald eagle (see eagle) **132**-10
beautiful **11**-21
big **11**-2
biking **159**-4
birds **132**
blue **12**-1
call 141-E
camping stoves **154**-16
canoeing **154**-3
canyon **117**-17
climb 153-C
day **18**-10
each day (see every day) **18**-21
fax 142-B
fishing **154**-6
foam pads **154**-13
forests **117**-11
green **12**-8
hike *v.* hiking **154**-6
hikers (see hiking) **154**-6
hiking **154**-6
July **19**-31
lakes **117**-13
lanterns **154**-22
jump 156-J
learn (see **learn** to drive) **28**-E
learn to drive **28**-E
miles **15**
moose **134**-1
mountains (see mountain range)
    117-15
physically challenged **22**-25
plane (see airplane) **110**-9
plants **128**
price **21**-2,3,6
race car (see sports car) **106**-6
rivers **117**-3
sailboarding **160**-10
schools **112**
scuba diving **160**-12
sheep **133**-7
ski adj. skiing **160**-1, 3

skiing **160**-1, 3
sleeping bags **154**-12
teach 140
tennis **159**-14
tents **154**-10
watch 27-S
waterfalls **117**-2
wild animals **133**

I Can!, p. 101

accident **102**-2
ball (see baseball) **161**-18
ball (see basketball) **161**-4
baseball **158**-9
basketball **158**-8
biking **159**-4
body **74**
boy **22**-7
catch 156-E
catcher *n.* (see **catch**) **156**-E
climbing *n.* **climb 153**-C
coach **158**-2
court **158**-7
dancing dance 33-J
difficult **11**-24
down (see sad) **31**-20
dribble 156-K
eleventh **14**
faster fast **11**-3
female **4**-14
hand **74**-8
hit 156-G
hours **16**-3
Japan **124-125**
kids (see children) **22**-1
legs **74**-6
loves (see in love) **30**-19
martial arts **159**-10
miles **15**
minutes **16**-2
pass 156-H
physical challenge *n.* physically
    challenged **22**-25
physically challenged **22**-25
play (see player) **158**-5
player **158**-5
racing *adj.* **race 157**-Y
race *n.*, racers (see **race**) **157**-Y
rafting **154**-4
ran run 156-C
run 156-C
scuba diving **160**-12
shooting *n.* **shoot 156**-I
skier (see **ski**) **157**-U
skiing **160**-1
slowly *adv.* slow **11**-4
sports **158**
street **90**-9
summer **19**-38
team **158**
throw 156-D
time **16-17**
tractor trailer **106**-15
United States **122-125**
winter **19**-40
woman **22**-10
won win 158
world **124-125**
wheelchair **80**-6
year **18**-8